OnlinePlumbingAdvice
.com

www.MikeQuick.com

OnlinePlumbingAdvice.com
How to find the best plumber, plumbing products and plumbing advice
By Mike Quick

Important Notice – Disclaimer

Published by Quick Quality Publishing Company
Printed in the United States of America

WWW.ONLINEPLUMBINGADVICE.COM

WWW.QUICKQUALITYPUBLISHING.COM

WWW.MIKEQUICK.COM

ISBN: 0982983905
ISBN-13: 9780982983904
LCCN: 2009909220

OnlinePlumbingAdvice.com

How to find the best plumber, plumbing products
and plumbing advice

Michael Quick

DEDICATION

This book is dedicated to my customers.

*I appreciate your trust in me; I appreciate the way
so many of you make me feel like part of your family.*

*As we grow old together and learn from one another,
as I meet your children and your grand children,
it makes me glad to be your family's plumber.*

⟲

Table of Contents

Introduction

About the Author

HELLO, I AM Mike Quick. I had good grades in college, but decided to be a plumber. I left college to begin my apprenticeship.

I started my plumbing apprenticeship in December of 1969. I was drafted into the U.S. Army in 1970 and discharged in 1972. Immediately following my honorable discharge, I continued my plumbing apprenticeship. I became a licensed journeymen plumber in 1977 and became a licensed master plumber and master gasfitter in 1980.

I started Quick Quality Plumbing and Heating (later to be known as Quick Quality Plumbing Inc.) in 1981.

A major nonprofit consumer-monitoring magazine in the Washington, D.C. and Northern Virginia area has provided very favorable ratings for Quick Quality Plumbing Inc. Since I began my business, my customers have consistently provided top satisfaction ratings for my work and their customer experience. I think my reputation should help you feel that I can be trusted, and my over thirty-eight years of experience makes me a trustworthy plumbing adviser.

Because of my experience, I can offer superior advice that can help you avoid plumbing mistakes. I have worked in commercial, industrial, medical, and other types of plumbing work, but my specialty has always been solving plumbing problems in the home. It is difficult to find a plumber with thirty-eight years of experience solving plumbing problems in homes. This makes me uniquely qualified to help you save money, avoid confusion, and make better plumbing decisions. I take pride in my work and have always strived to do my best for every customer. As I wrote this book, I strived to provide advice that will help you avoid plumbing mistakes.

As you focus on the details of my qualifications, I think you will see that I can help you focus on important details concerning plumbers, plumbing advice, and plumbing products. One of the most important factors to consider as you focus on my qualifications is my reputation for honesty. My plumbing business has always focused on being honest with my customers. I think my thirty-eight years of experience and my consistently high customer satisfaction ratings provide evidence that I have always been honest with my customers. I am worthy of your trust. You can research claims I make. I want you to consider me as one of your trustworthy plumbing advisers.

As you read this book, you will see that I use the word trustworthy often. Trustworthy indicates that a person is actually worthy of your trust. If you just think he seems to be trustworthy, he sounds trustworthy, he looks trustworthy or he talked you into trusting him, he is not necessarily trustworthy. To actually be trustworthy, you have to check the plumber's specialized qualifications and reputation for honesty. Neighbors often know which plumbers have a good reputation; sometimes non-profit consumer groups collect opinions from consumers. Always try to do as much research as you can to find a trustworthy plumber. Plumbers that specialize in the type of plumbing work you need and have the best reputation, are usually trustworthy.

The key to finding trustworthy plumbing products is gathering recommendations from trustworthy plumbers and trustworthy plumbing advisers. Plumbers that specialize in plumbing inside the home are usually your best source for advice concerning plumbing products in the home (plumbers that fix problems in the home are usually aware of what products have the most problems).

I often see defects in plumbing products, poorly designed plumbing products, and poorly installed products. I have noticed many major plumbing problems that could have been avoided if home owners, property managers, designers, and other professionals based decisions on trustworthy advice. It's my hope that my knowledge and experience can help you gather trustworthy advice. By focusing on the most frequently occurring mistakes, I can help you avoid major plumbing problems.

In preparation for this book, I began taking notes over two decades ago. My observations concerning important but often overlooked details and other costly mistakes are included in this book. My notes, experience, research, and knowledge provide a unique opportunity for you to gather trustworthy plumbing advice.

I could tell you that I am so smart that I can give you simple easy answers to all your plumbing problems. I could tell you that I can show you an easy simple way for you or anyone to do plumbing. I could promote false promises and sell lots of books-like many others did. That would probably be very profitable-short term.

It wouldn't be honest, and it wouldn't be good long-term. Because so many have made so much by oversimplifying and misleading, this first book has to deal with convincing you to focus on details. Some details might seem boring. You might skip through some of this book. I plan to publish more books, long-term, my honest approach worked for my plumbing business and I hope, with your help, it will work for my publishing business.

About This Book

I THINK THIS BOOK will greatly improve the quality of information you use when making important plumbing decisions. The advice contained in this book is based on my opinions (my interpretation of what I observed). One of the most important elements of my job is providing plumbing advice for my customers. The same skills are important in this book. I try to provide advice before, during, and, after I do work for my customers. In this book I try to let you benefit from the same advice I give my customers. I hope that my advice will help you avoid problems, make better decisions, and understand whether or not you are dealing with the best available plumber. I always focus on what I think provides the best chance of the best, most cost-effective, long-term results.

Properly installed and properly maintained plumbing is very important. Your family's health is directly affected by the quality of your plumbing. People seem to forget that the primary function of plumbing is to provide sanitation. Properly installed and properly maintained plumbing protects your family from the many dangerous organic and nonorganic substances inside and outside your home.

Improperly installed or improperly maintained plumbing inside your home is more dangerous than no plumbing. Leaky plumbing can create unsanitary conditions by providing a pathway for dangerous contaminants. Leaky plumbing can also provide a breeding ground for **dangerous mold, insects, mice, and other organisms.**

Providing a sanitary environment is the most important function of plumbing. Proper installation and proper maintenance is essential for reliable plumbing.

To enjoy the benefits of sanitary living conditions in your home, you must focus on the **best long-term solutions** for plumbing problems. The best long-term solutions require the best plumbing decisions. One of the most important decisions takes place when you select plumbing products. Proper research before you select plumbing products can help avoid serious reoccurring problems later. Usually, you will need the help of the best plumber and the best plumbing advisers to properly research plumbing products and make your best plumbing decisions.

The biggest problem facing people today is finding trustworthy advice. It is easy to get advice, but it is difficult to get trustworthy, truly expert advice. Place the proper amount of value on advice and you will avoid lots of confusion. Qualify experts before you invest your time, and you can gather trustworthy advice efficiently while you avoid overwhelming confusion. This book will help you find trustworthy advice.

My reputation and my more than thirty-eight years of specialized plumbing experience make me uniquely qualified to be one of your best trustworthy plumbing advisers. My plumbing specialty is solving plumbing problems in the home, and **this book is about solving and avoiding plumbing problems in the home.**

This book should provide one of your best sources of **top quality plumbing research**. Important decisions should be based on honest, truly qualified expert advice. The primary focus of this book is to help you do research. There are sections intended to answer questions, help improve media content, manufacturer's product development, and other related matters. All of these sections are focused on improving the quality of plumbing in the home.

Unlike many books, this book offers possible solutions for most of the problems I illustrate. Overly simplified, misleading, and sometimes incorrect media productions can improve. Manufacturers can develop better products. Home owners can make better plumbing decisions. This book contains advice that can improve media content and improve product development. As home owners learn to place the proper amount of value on advice and learn how to select quality plumbing products, they will improve the sanitation in their homes, save money and avoid aggravation.

This book not only provides advice that can help you avoid mistakes, it also offers advice to help you find mistakes. By learning secrets concerning what to do before a plumber arrives, while the plumber is at your home, and what to do after the plumber leaves, you can avoid many costly, unhealthy, and aggravating problems.

Don't Expect Perfect Text from a Plumber

I HESITATED BEFORE INCLUDING this section because many people might think it is arrogant for me to suggest that readers adjust to a plumber's style. People need to realize that most skilled tradesmen find it difficult to provide perfectly prepared text, so I decided that I must provide this section.

It is easy to find perfectly produced text. It is almost impossible to find perfectly produced text provided by a plumber, electrician, tile man, carpenter, or other skilled craftsmen. As I write this book, I plan to help other trustworthy skilled craftsmen write books. I hope that readers will learn to realize that top-quality writing style is not as important as top-quality content.

As you learn to focus on honest, specialized, expert advice (based on expert opinion), you might have to put a little more effort into adjusting to the expert's style. But, before I explain what I mean by that, I need to clarify something. *Specialized expert* might seem like a waste of words or redundant to some people. There's a reason why I use two words to describe an expert.

Most people consider a master plumber a plumbing expert. A master plumber that specializes in one type of plumbing would be considered a *specialized expert* in that type of plumbing (for example, piping new homes, maintenance and repair of homes, commercial maintenance and repair, etc.) If people think of plumbing specialists as they think of medical doctor specialists, they might begin to understand how important specialized experience and knowledge is. When you have a problem with your hand, the medical opinions of a hand specialist are far more valuable than that of a primary care medical doctor. Usually, the opinions of a well-established, highly regarded hand specialist are more valuable than that of other less experienced hand specialists. Communicating with the best hand specialist might require more effort on your part, but it would be well worth the effort.

I am a master plumber who specializes in home plumbing problems. You might have to adjust to my style of writing, but my plumbing experience will make your efforts well worth it. Please believe me when I tell you that I have read many books concerning writing, publishing, and communicating. I have hired people to help me, and I reached the point where I realize that no author is perfect. I hope my basic style presents my specialized expert opinions clearly. This is my first book, and I believe that my honest specialized expert opinion is far more important than fancy perfection. With your help, my next book will be better.

How to Use This Book

MOST PEOPLE WILL probably quickly scan the information in this book and focus on their most urgent concerns as they find time. All readers are strongly advised to read all disclaimers before they read anything else. Disclaimers are the most important part to read.

The second most important part of the book to read is About the Author. I always say that people must check out the qualifications and reputation of an expert before placing any value on the expert's opinion.

After reading the most important parts of this book, jumping around to topics of interest might be the best way to gather timely information concerning my opinions. It is always recommended that you gather the opinions of as many trustworthy experts as your time will allow.

How you do research in the amount of time that you have available will have a profound effect on the quality of the decisions you make. After you focus on the most urgent concerns, I think you'll find it beneficial to read the whole book.

Caution: Jumping around to topics you most urgently need is not the same as failing to read important details. After you jump to a topic, you should read all the details concerning that topic. Rushing through a topic and perhaps missing important details, might give you a false impression.

Often problems can be avoided if you understand important details and how these details affect the frequency of malfunctions. I try to provide ways that many frequently occurring problems can be avoided. Learning from others' mistakes can save you lots of time, money, and aggravation.

This book will provide instant answers for many of your immediate plumbing concerns. As you find time to read through it, this book can help you develop a plumbing problem prevention plan. You will quickly learn to keep this book available for future reference as other problems develop. I hope that you will buy extra copies for your friends and relatives.

CHAPTER 1

Avoid Overwhelming Confusion

Why People Get Confused

IT'S IMPORTANT TO learn to tell the difference between a plumber that focuses on your best interest and a plumber that focuses on his best interest. If you understand why plumbers do business the way they do, you will be less confused and learn to spot the plumber with your best interest in mind.

Listening to customers is one of the most important parts of my job. Noting what customers say and how they say it helps me focus on what I need to say. After I answer questions, I listen to the customer's response. I try to determine if customers understand my advice. I try to adjust my communication skills to fit each customer. As I write this book, I'm focusing on what I learned from talking to my customers and especially on what were their most frequent problems. I think the majority of the readers need to know that **misplaced trust** and **failure to identify experts** often results in major long-term problems. I find it disturbing that in recent years, most people seem to make plumbing decisions based on less than trustworthy advice.

Plumbing is not as simple or easy as many people think. It's important to take a more serious look at plumbing and focus on the long-term consequences of overlooking small details.

If plumbing work was as simple as it is often portrayed on television and other media, it wouldn't matter who did it. It wouldn't matter which plumber you use or even if you did it yourself. If boring, time-consuming, details weren't important, it wouldn't matter if you based your plumbing decisions on misleading entertainment. The truth is the details are important and decisions should be based on quality research.

The power of the media to make things seem simple and easy to do is entertaining. People want simple, easy ways to solve problems. Entertainment is designed to give people what they want. The easy-how- to -do it entertainment trend seems to distract people from doing quality research.

If reliable plumbing and sanitation weren't so important this misguided trend wouldn't be so dangerous. If satisfactory *long-term results* didn't rely on often overlooked details, overlooked details wouldn't matter.

Many people oversimplify plumbing and fail to understand that all plumbers are not the same (many are not even real plumbers). People who assume all plumbers are equally skilled and equally honest enjoy price shopping for plumbers but often learn the mistake of this approach the hard way. These same people expect a plumber to offer round-the-clock availability. This is a big mistake that they typically learn after major problems occur.

You can avoid lots of problems, if you research plumbers before they come to your home. Focus on the qualifications of the plumber and the amount of time the plumber works at your home. Focus on paying for what you get. Don't expect the best plumbers to be on standby twenty-four/seven or to waste a lot of time guessing how much time it will take to do small plumbing jobs.

When people call me to ask about prices, less than three of every one hundred callers ask about the qualifications of the person who will do the work. When I explain the difference between a technician, an installer, and a plumber, they usually seem uninterested. Many people seem to expect convenient or immediate after-hours scheduling. These people don't seem to realize that most good plumbers need to schedule work during normal business hours.

Sadly, many people fail to understand the value of journeymen plumbers and master plumbers who have worked in the trade many years and successfully passed a plumbing test. All journeymen plumbers and master plumbers are not equally honest or equally qualified, but some focus on qualifications is better than none. As customers fail to realize that all plumbers are not the same, the quality of their plumbing will suffer. The frequency of emergency plumbing problems will increase, and over time these people will learn how important good plumbers are.

There is a major shortage of trustworthy plumbers. People are beginning to realize that bad plumbing causes mold problems, health problems, and other very dangerous problems. Long-term sanitary living conditions in your home will depend on your ability to find a trustworthy plumber. Finding, communicating with, and building a mutually beneficial relationship with a trustworthy plumber will make you an established customer. Many trustworthy plumbers only accept a limited number of new customers, so the sooner you become a new customer, the faster you become an established customer. It is important that you learn to focus properly as you search for a trustworthy plumber.

Focus on qualifications and reputation as you shop for a good plumber. Learn to avoid emergency situations by properly maintaining your plumbing. If it's difficult for you to leave work to meet a plumber at your house during regular business hours, find a church member, family member, or friend who can. Consider hiring a property manager or other professional to help find and/or meet plumbers and other tradesmen as needed.

Quality plumbing repairs will help you avoid future problems. Low-quality, convenient repairs today could result in untimely, inconvenient problems tomorrow. Bargain shopping for small plumbing work usually ends up with you paying more for less. Focus on the quality of the plumber and the amount of time he works at your home. Work, promises, and prices are only valuable if provided by a trustworthy plumber.

A Checklist for Determining the Value of a Plumber

DETERMINE IF THE person who will show up at your home and do the work:

- ☐ Is a properly licensed journeyman or master plumber

- ☐ Specializes in the type of plumbing work you need

- ☐ Has an established reputation—good or bad

- ☐ Is properly insured

This checklist, any other research you can do, and talking to neighbors should help you avoid costly, aggravating mistakes.

Media Problems: "Garbage In, Garbage Out"

MONITOR AS MUCH plumbing advice for home owners as I can. I review plumbing books, television shows, radio shows, and other media. I often see major defects in perfectly produced television shows and other media. If I rarely or infrequently noticed major defects, I wouldn't be concerned. The fact that I often see defects is disturbing. It seems that defective plumbing advice often gets recycled. Producers seem to find better ways to present the same bad information.

Sometimes, obsolete, over simplified, misleading, inaccurate advice produced in one form of media gets reproduced. I call that "garbage in, garbage out." Usually it is impossible to determine who the original "expert" was. As people see the same "expert" advice reproduced, they place even more confidence in the bad advice. This recycled bad advice is one of the biggest defects I see in the media.

Media producers that list the source of "expert" advice can help people determine the value of the advice. Often producers consult the wrong "experts" or fail to consult a specialized expert. I hope this book will convince media producers to look more carefully at "experts." If producers chose to reproduce information, they should identify the original "expert." By focusing more carefully on "experts," media producers can avoid the problem of garbage in, garbage out.

People need quality plumbing advice, and media producers can help. Producers can focus on top-quality sources of plumbing advice and produce truly top-quality media products.

It is amazing how much power perfectly produced media has.

Do Not Learn Just Enough to Get in Trouble

PEOPLE SEEM TO think plumbing is so simple that it doesn't matter which plumber they hire. Some people even try to do it themselves. Eventually they learn that this is a big mistake. A small plumbing problem can easily become a major problem if not handled properly. Before people make important plumbing decisions, they need to make sure their decisions are based on reliable information, and they need enough information to avoid unnecessary risk.

As people learn to understand that quality content is more important than quality production, I think that honest, specialized experts will receive the respect and appreciation they deserve. Specialized experts should control the quality and amount of the content. Specialized experts can improve the quality of media production by making sure the production contains necessary, important details. As media production becomes more focused on quality content, people will make better plumbing decisions and enjoy the benefits of their quality research.

A Checklist to Help You Determine the Value of Media Productions

USING THE FOLLOWING checklist should help you focus properly on media productions.

- ☐ Try to determine the qualifications of the expert providing technical advice

- ☐ Try to determine if the focus is on entertainment or honest advice

- ☐ Is there any focus on possible complications

- ☐ Are there enough details

You Might Understand Why I Wrote This Book If You Ever:

- Realized that the plumber protects your family from unhealthy living conditions.

- Got overwhelmed by too many different answers to the same question.

- Realized that it is easy to get plumbing advice but difficult to get trustworthy plumbing advice.

- Thought you were getting a good deal but later found problems with pricing and/or workmanship.

- Started a do-it-yourself project and later realized that you were misled about how simple and easy it would be.

- Thought you saved lots of money by doing it yourself, but months or years later experienced a flood or other major problem because of a detail that you overlooked.

- Thought you saved lots of money, by getting competitive bids, but months or years later experienced a flood or other major problem because of an overlooked detail.

- Thought you avoided staying home from work and waiting for a plumber, by finding a more convenient plumber, but months or years later experienced a flood or other major problem because of an overlooked detail.

- Felt like a plumber wasn't providing a simple, easy-to-understand answer to what you thought was a simple question.

You Might Understand Why I Wrote This Book If You Ever Wondered Why:

- Most estimates, set prices, and firm prices are subject to change.

- Some plumbers seem to take the approach that the customer is always right and some don't.

- Some plumbers provide an almost endless supply of guarantees and some don't.

- It is difficult to find a good plumber.

- It is difficult to find trustworthy advice.

- It is difficult to find quality plumbing products.

- Plumbing parts are often difficult to find.

- Some plumbers don't have needed parts.

- Plumbing doesn't seem to hold up as well as it use to.

Media Production: Two Types of Experts

THIS SECTION MIGHT **seem to be more about media production and less about plumbing. It is presented as an additional effort to illustrate why people often get misled and confused as they try to find trustworthy plumbing advice.**

When I started studying book production, I learned that there are two basic types of people producing expert advice. A specialized expert often uses his knowledge and research to produce advice. I call this **expert advice provided directly from the expert**. A second source of expert advice is available from people who specialize in gathering expert advice. I call this **expert advice that is**

produced by a research expert. Before investing your time gathering advice, I recommend investing time to determine if the expert is trustworthy.

When expert advice is provided directly from the expert, researching the expert should help you determine the value of the advice.

When expert advice is provided by a research expert, focus carefully on the source of the expert advice. If a research expert fails to list the source of the expert opinions, I recommend that you place very little or no value on the advice. Sometimes research experts list the source in general terms such as a plumber or a builder; I consider that of little value. If you wish to avoid confusion and rely on specialized expert advice, you must always identify the specialized expert.

I think that when book producers, magazine producers, or, other media producers gather expert advice, they should always list the experts. As people realize how important trustworthy content is, I think producers will have to.

This Checklist for Plumbing Research should help you avoid mistakes that many others make.

Checklist for Plumbing Research

As you collect plumbing advice always try to determine if the expert:

- ☐ Gathers expert advice or is the expert

- ☐ Has superior specialized qualifications and experience

- ☐ Has an established reputation

- ☐ Is just selling a product

- ☐ Is focused on entertainment or your best interest

Expert advice that is produced by a research expert falls into two basic groups. One group provides the source of the expert advice (where they found the advice) and the other group does not. I recommend focusing on the group that tells you where they got the expert advice because you can only check experts if you know their names. I recommend that people avoid advice that has been recycled from unknown or less than trustworthy sources.

CHAPTER 2

Learn from Others' Mistakes

What is more important?
What you get or what you think you are getting?

I USE TO BELIEVE that if a person could invent a better mousetrap (hopefully a humane mousetrap) he could make millions of dollars. Now it seems that presentation, marketing, and promotion are more important than the quality of a product. Properly promoted, poorly designed mousetraps like properly promoted bad plumbing services, can make lots of money. **Sadly, it doesn't seem to matter what customers get, what matters is what they think they are getting.**

People often think they are getting:

- A free estimate

- An easy way to compare prices

- An easy way to keep plumbers honest

- An easy way to know if a plumber knows what he is doing

- An easy way to compare promises, conveniences, and guarantees

Some plumbing businesses and other businesses make lots of money only because they play tricks on consumers. Marketing and promotion tricks can make consumers think they are getting a bargain. A 100 percent customer satisfaction guarantee seems to remove all risk, but it doesn't. A 100 percent low-price guarantee seems to guarantee a low price, but it doesn't. Most people learn the hard way, but you don't have to.

There is **a secret** way to watch for this type of trick. Usually everything the customer wants is printed in large easy-to-read print. Most information concerning details that make the difference between a good deal and a bad one are in small print. Many years ago, business often ran on honest promises and a handshake. Many years ago, fine print didn't matter much. These days, most businesses run on fine print, and customers must be very careful if they want to understand what they are getting.

High-profit companies focus on providing customers what they want. First, most customers want full control. Second, they want a reasonable price. Third, they want promises and guarantees. All these elements, presented in an enjoyable way often make the difference between a high-profit business and no business. Keep things simple, mislead, and protect your business with the right fine print, and big profits can be made.

The qualifications of the worker, the amount of time he works in the home, seem unimportant as long as customers **think** they are getting what they want. Usually, these high-profit companies offer guarantees that **seem** to protect customers. One-year guarantees are usually no problem for the business since major problems often take more than a year to become obvious.

The secret is detailed research. You must establish the trustworthiness of a business before you trust them. Prices, promises, guarantees, and fine print are not as important as those that provide them. The best, most honest business might use the same fine print as a questionable business, but the fine print is often used in a much different way. If you want to get what you pay for, focus on finding a trustworthy business. Talk to neighbors and find other ways to find a trustworthy plumber.

A trustworthy business wants to provide a qualified plumber at a reasonable labor rate—no more, no less. A trustworthy business doesn't want to play misleading games or make unrealistic promises.

Most trustworthy plumbers will not waste time with customers that fail to understand that it is not cost effective to estimate small plumbing jobs because there are too many possible complications that could dramatically increase or decrease the price. If a trustworthy plumber provides a high price to include some possible complications that may occur, he might have to increase the price by 100 percent. After doubling the price, a trustworthy plumber would have four things to worry about:

1. After providing a price for a small job, there is always a possibility that a major complication could be discovered that could result in a 200 percent or more increase in price.

2. After providing a price that was double what will probably be required, a customer could use that amount to say the trustworthy plumber tried to cheat him.

3. If no complications occur, and the work is completed in the normal amount of time, some customers would feel cheated.

4. If the work goes even more smoothly and easily than normal, some customers would feel even more cheated.

Most trustworthy plumbers find it impossible to get most people to understand the difference between high-quality work and low-quality work. Even when the amount of work is exactly the same, the quality can be dramatically different. This helps low-quality; less-than-trustworthy plumbing businesses enjoy larger profits. Trustworthy plumbers are often expected to provide top quality work at prices offered by less than trustworthy plumbing businesses.

Years ago, less than trustworthy businesses use to get customers by offering lower prices than trustworthy plumbing businesses; these days, higher prices are often the norm. People seem to favor businesses that sell promises and convenience. People don't mind paying extra-as long as they think they are getting what they want. This is another type of shopping. I call this shopping for convenience and promises.

Because of the recent focus on shopping, people often lose sight of what's really important-that a qualified expert actually corrects the problem. People think they are paying to have a problem solved, and once it's solved, they think they can feel confident that the plumber will guarantee the problem will not return. People think that because they're paying to have the problem solved, who solves the problem, when they solve it, and how much it costs is not important. Most people seem to think what they are getting is a promise that their problem will be solved once and for all.

Most people seem to fail to understand that in the real world, life is not that simple. When people pay for the services of a plumber or pay for the services of a medical specialist, they are paying for the time a qualified specialist works to solve a problem. Sometimes an honest effort by a highly qualified specialist will fail to solve a problem. Unfortunately, the latest trend has been to blame the specialist for any undesirable results and assume the specialist made a mistake. Most people seem to think that promises and guarantees are the most important element of doing business. Dishonest business people find it easy to offer promises and guarantees, but honest business people have to deal with the real world. In the real world, the best attempt performed by the best specialist will not always provide the best results.

When an honest, highly qualified plumber applies his skills to solve a problem, people usually will enjoy their most cost-effective, long-term solution for the problem. Guarantees and promises are fine, but when they are carefully applied to replace quality plumbing work and to distract people from what is most important, they become tools of destruction.

Long-term results and sanitary living conditions suffer when you follow trends and fail to understand what you are getting for your money. You should always focus on what is really important and on who will show up at your home to help solve your problem. Money paid for an honest qualified plumber's time is money well spent. Money paid for promises is often wasted.

Now, I hope you understand the difference between really getting what you want and just thinking you are getting what you want.

If you want to avoid misleading tricks, you must:

- Establish trust before you believe guarantees and other promises

- Focus properly on what you are getting for your money

- Don't let tricky marketing distract you

- Read all fine print

Focus on Details

WHEN I STARTED writing this book, I decided that I should focus on what I see as the most urgent and most frequently occurring problem that seems to cause the largest percentage of unsanitary living conditions.

At first I thought toilet problems like poorly installed toilets and weak-flushing toilets should be my first priority. After I wrote many pages about toilet problems, I realized that toilet problems are not the most urgent problem. **The most urgent plumbing problem is that people fail to understand the importance of details.** I hope I can get people to realize how important reliable plumbing is. I hope people can learn to realize that properly installed and properly maintained plumbing protects their family's health. If people understand that reliable, sanitary plumbing protects the health of their family, they will see how important it is to focus on details.

The secret can be found in the details.

Details, concerning **who people trust for advice**, greatly affect important plumbing decisions. **Details** concerning **how they select plumbing products** greatly affect the long-term sanitation of their home. **Details** concerning who they allow to do plumbing work in their home and **details** concerning how the work is done also greatly affect the long-term sanitation of their home.

If details weren't important, it wouldn't matter who provided plumbing advice. **If** details weren't important, it wouldn't matter who did plumbing work in your home.

If details weren't important you could call the most convenient plumber and never have to take off work to wait for a plumber.

If details weren't important, all plumbing products would be equally durable and reliable.

If small but important details didn't make the difference between sanitary and unsanitary long-term results, these details wouldn't matter.

As you read this book, you will see that I provide many helpful details and I also provide ways for you to research important details.

The purpose of this book is to save you time, money, and aggravation as you solve plumbing problems and try to avoid future problems

Some benefits of this book include:

- Research time will be kept to a minimum as you learn to check out the experts' qualifications and reputation before you invest your time.

- Learning how to find the best available plumber before you need one will save lots of time later. Make sure the plumber is worth waiting for and avoid reoccurring problems.

- Developing efficient communication between you and the plumber will save everyone lots of time and make you one of his best customers.

- You will learn how to avoid mistakes.

- You will learn what to do after you make a mistake.

- You will learn how to benefit from your mistakes.

CHAPTER 3

Secrets Concerning Different Business Models

Understanding Different Business Models

ONE OF THE most common plumbing business models seems to provide the best chance of making big profits. Like other big business models, it involves focusing on playing the competitive game and providing the best possible image. Often, image building by expert marketing and other promotional services is so good that prices and quality don't seem to mater. I am not saying that all plumbing businesses that use this model are dishonest, misleading, and/or provide low-quality services—I am saying be careful.

It just seems to me that giving customers what they want, when they want it usually results in higher prices for lower quality. Prices have to be inflated and "standby" plumbers are usually not the best.

Many large plumbing companies seem to provide products and services in a way designed to attract the largest amount of business.

They advertise and do whatever it takes to find new customers. They don't seem to be concerned if customers think they were charged too much or were provided low-quality services because new customers will replace them.

Imaginary Bargain Prices:

- **"Free" estimates** (AKA "fixed Prices") even for very small jobs. This practice makes it easy for customers to bargain shop. Most people seem to think estimates keep plumbers honest by creating competition.

  Secret: There is no such thing as a free estimate. Often, the estimate is **only "free" if you accept the estimate.** In that case, the cost of the estimate is built into the price quoted. When estimates are freely offered with **no obligations,** the cost of the **"free"** estimate **is still built into** the prices provided. If you don't accept the price and let the estimator do the work, expenses are passed on to the people that do. I once had a boss who figured we would get one out of three free-estimated jobs. He said the one person who used his plumbing services would pay for the lost time providing the other two estimates. After the expenses for a "free" estimate were figured, the amount was multiplied by three; unconditional "free" estimates cost more than the other type.

- **Coupons and other discounts** attract attention and seem to provide high value at a special price.

  Secret: Promotion, printing, and additional necessary processing expenses are **eventually built into the price** customers pay. People seem to enjoy gimmicks and games, but most people don't seem to understand that **fancy features cost money.**

- **Credit cards that provide rewards and added consumer protection** also make payment more convenient. Some credit cards even add an extra layer of dispute resolution in case the consumer is not satisfied with the services provided. As long as the consumer pays the credit card company within thirty days, all these added features seem to cost nothing and appear to be a real bargain.

  <u>Secret:</u> **All these features cost money.** Most credit cards add more than 2 percent of the charged amount in expenses for the plumbing business. Processing transactions usually costs even more. Exposure to extra layers of consumer protection adds additional expense. Dishonest, unreasonable consumers can use well-intended, consumer protection unfairly. Guilty until proven innocent type allegations, manufactured stories and other time-consuming disputes increase risk and expenses. Plumbers fear unfair judgment more than anything. Credit card resolution specialists have the ability to make judgments that can damage good reputations. **If a careless judgment damages a good reputation, it can be very expensive and time-consuming to repair.**

Imaginary Protection from Low-Quality Services and Mistakes

<u>Secret:</u> Dishonest or misleading plumbers **often** offer promises and guarantees that are **not enforceable and are not realistic.** Promises and guarantees are often made worthless by fine print that is overlooked. **Promises and guarantees have value only when plumbers are trustworthy.**

Should you expect the best plumbers to be the most convenient?

- **Most people find it difficult to take off work to wait for a plumber**. Many large plumbing companies keep plumbers on standby duty (available twenty-four/seven).

  <u>Secret:</u> **Most of the best plumbers do not work weekends, holidays, or evenings.** Most of the best plumbers stay busy during regular business hours. Being on call or trying to provide round-the-clock plumbing services can be harmful to a plumber's health and/or family life.

- **Emergency plumbing problems often occur on holidays, weekends, and late in the evening.** Most large plumbing companies expect some of their plumbers to be available for these emergencies.

  <u>Secret:</u> **Most of the best plumbers try to squeeze emergency plumbing work in during regular business hours**. Sometimes they will work late to accommodate these jobs. When customers experience emergencies, they often have to be happy with whatever plumber they can get in a timely manner. When uncontrolled water is creating a risk of electrical shock or other **dangerous situations, sometimes the fire department might help.** Some areas recommend that callers use the nonemergency fire department phone number. Usually, this emergency response is to **get the water safely under control. Most emergency situations can be avoided** by keeping your plumbing properly maintained and by making sure plumbing work is only performed by a properly licensed, trustworthy plumber. Learning how to turn off water effectively can also help.

The following business model is the one I use and the one that most plumbing companies for which I worked used. It is much different than the model I just described above.

Quality Plumbing Services at a Reasonable Price: Avoid Unnecessary Expenses:

THIS SECOND BUSINESS **model is focused on retaining customers and building a mutually trusting relationship.** Trust works both ways—plumbers appreciate honest customers as much as customers appreciate honest plumbers.

☐ Make sure the customer gets what he pays for.

☐ Don't waste time trying to estimate small plumbing jobs. When complications could easily cost more than the estimate, it is usually not cost effective to try to estimate. When talking about possible complications can easily take more time than the work is likely to take, it is not cost effective to estimate.

☐ Try to avoid undesirable customers that seem to have unrealistic expectations.

☐ Try to communicate with customers before, during, and after providing plumbing services. When reasonably possible and cost effective, try to explain options, risks, and details.

☐ Avoid wasting time and money on coupons, bargain discounts, credit cards, and other marketing tools and pass this savings on to the customers.

☐ On big jobs make a reasonable effort to provide a competitive price for quality products and services. Try to explain important details that make the difference between quality and promises of quality. Try to explain that all plumbers and all plumbing work is not the same.

Avoid competition that compares corner-cutting dishonest plumbers to your honest, top-quality products and services.

☐ After completing contracted jobs, total the amount of hours spent on the job and see if the price was figured accurately. Be aware that figuring too much labor is just as bad as not figuring enough.

☐ Build the customer base by establishing a good reputation and relying primarily on customers recommending your plumbing services based on their experience.

Secret: Establishing credibility and trust is the key to the best long-term business plan.

Large plumbing jobs provide the opportunity for contracts, detailed biding, and other time-consuming aspects of doing business. Large projects often can absorb or limit extra charges for unexpected complications (usually 10 percent or less additional charges).

Plumbing jobs that are likely to cost less than $700.00 (if there are no complications) are what I consider small jobs. As I mentioned earlier, it's actually more difficult to provide an estimate for a small job because unexpected complications can increase the cost by more than 100 percent and explaining possible complications can take more time than the actual work.

Honest, trustworthy plumbers realize that complications can occur at any time, and because of this, they are often uncomfortable presenting prices or estimates for small jobs. (There are so many possible complications that can develop at any time, that it is impossible to discuss them all.) People often feel uncomfortable when this type of plumber tries to explain possible complications. Many people say the plumber was "talking the job to death" or "I don't trust plumbers that don't give a set price." These days many plumbers are being forced to estimate all plumbing work or perish.

I don't try to estimate small plumbing jobs. Because I specialize in small jobs, most of my customers pay for the actual time I spend solving their problems, and for the parts I supply (AKA time and material). I provide honest highly qualified plumbing services at a lower rate than most in my area. I consider that a bargain. My way of doing business gives customers the best value because they only pay for what they get, and when no complications pop up, they usually get a super bargain.

My honesty and experience keep complications to a minimum. Experienced plumbers know ways to disturb surrounding fittings as little as possible, and an honest effort provides the best chance of avoiding complications. Most of my customers know me and trust me; they seem to appreciate me, and I appreciate them.

Some honest trustworthy plumbers try to estimate small jobs. They usually explain that if they provide a price, it will usually be much higher than it normally would cost (i.e., double the normal no complication price). They explain that additional charges still might be necessary if any extreme complications develop. There are many variations on how plumbers charge for complications. Basically trustworthy plumbers try to be as fair as possible with their pricing.

Many less-than-trustworthy plumbers like to estimate all plumbing work. By providing an estimate, they can justify charging outrageous prices while providing low-quality work. It is important to realize what you are purchasing. If you get a sales pitch and agree to a price, you are choosing to agree to the terms- and- probably providing a way for the salesman/plumber to justify the price.

You might never realize what you paid for unless you:

1. Establish the qualifications of the plumber.

2. Establish what complications are included in the price.

3. Keep track of how long the plumber works on the job.

Some ways to tell if you made a mistake:

- After the workmen leaves, you realize that you paid for three hours of labor, but only got one hour.

- You find out that you paid the going rate for a journeymen or master plumber in your area but found out the person who did the work was not a plumber.

- You experience major problems later (often years later) attributable to defective work.

- Complications developed that cost you extra money and now you are wondering if the complication was caused by negligence, lack of experience, carelessness, or deliberately created to increase the price.

- You find that the worker failed to advise you about a major problem he should have noticed.

- Later you find out that a trustworthy plumber could have done the work for 50 percent less and the work would have been worthy of your long-term trust.

- Later you find out the corner-cutting work you paid for will result in long-term problems.

In summary:

Many people want an estimate or a set price and think all plumbers are equally honest and will provide the same quality of work. This type of shopping provides a major advantage to dishonest plumbers and those who are not even real plumbers. Set prices are usually high and prices can change; promises and guarantees that come easy are usually of little value. Often, these shoppers who focus on price end up paying more than they should have and usually lose even more when serious problems begin popping up. Later in this book I provide more details concerning misguided shopping and the long-term effect on the quality of the plumbing trade. You can save money by dealing with a trustworthy plumber. A dishonest plumber will often provide low-quality services at a high price.

Try to Schedule Work During Normal Business Hours

ALWAYS TRY TO get plumbing work performed during regular scheduled business hours. The plumber who comes to your home after normal hours is not likely to be among the best.

Waiting for the best trustworthy plumber is usually time well spent. His expert help will provide you with the best chance of avoiding complications now and in the future. I continue to be amazed at the people who wonder why the plumber they waited for all day Sunday charged lots of money and did a lousy job. Plumbing that is properly maintained by a trustworthy plumber is your best way to avoid emergency situations and aggravation. Normally, the best plumbers need to schedule work; most trustworthy plumbers are not sitting around waiting for the phone to ring.

When you read my section on Avoiding Emergency Situations, you will see how important a top-quality plumber is. You will see how bad decisions today will result in emergencies in the future. You will quickly learn how important top- quality plumbing advice is.

A Checklist to Help Expose Misleading Business Practices

To FOCUS ON honest businesses, focus on:

☐ Fine print

☐ Reputation

☐ Realistic expectations

☐ The true value of promises and guarantees

☐ Actual time a specialist works on your problem

Use this checklist and always expect to get no more than what you pay for. This provides your best chance of getting what you paid for. This honest approach provides the best chance of the best long-term results.

CHAPTER 4

The Best Way to Search for the Best Plumber

Communication and Searching for the Best Plumber

GOOD TRUSTWORTHY PLUMBERS are getting hard to find, so before you call one, I want to provide some guidelines that should help you start off on the right foot. **Secret:** Most people don't realize it, but most top-quality plumbers have invested many years building a good reputation and try to be careful in who they work for. Some tradesmen call this "qualifying the customer" (or you could call it disqualifying the customer). If all plumbers were the same, it wouldn't mater how you talked to a plumber. Trustworthy plumbers want trustworthy customers. Most less than trustworthy plumbers want any customers they can get.

Trustworthy customers must have reasonable expectations. Unreasonable expectations can come in many forms. Talking for a half hour on the phone about a plumbing repair that might take fifteen minutes might be unreasonable. Replacing a whole bathroom or some other big job allows for lengthy discussion, but small jobs must be scheduled efficiently. [Note: I provide details concerning this problem later in the book.]

Communication is important. If you organize what you want to tell a plumber, before you call, it can save time and aggravation. I've put together a list of dos and don'ts that might help you.

Do provide a brief description of your plumbing problem (stick with the facts).

Example: I found a puddle of water around my water heater.

Don't speculate about the cause and make statements that might be incorrect.

Example: My water heater is leaking.

I used this example because I have dealt with people who called me shopping for a water heater because they assumed it was leaking when it wasn't. Sometimes the air conditioner drain is stopped up, or the floor drain is stopped up or some other problem is causing the puddle.

Now I will illustrate another situation:

You noticed a drip in your ceiling, and you are searching for a plumber to fix it.

Do allow the plumber to ask questions and control the conversation.

Example: He might ask when you first noticed the problem and how fast is it dripping? Does the rate of dripping seem to be faster or slower since you first noticed it?

Don't consider it rude behavior if the plumber interrupts you as you try to control the conversation. Remember that the plumber wants to focus on important information that is needed to provide the best advice.

Example: As you try to tell him what you think the problem is-based on something you saw on television or based on what a clerk working at the hardware center thinks it is, he interrupts you and seems aggravated.

Explanation:

Most qualified plumbers prefer to focus on the facts in a timely manner. Wasting time discussing what you think it could be is disrespectful of the plumber's time. If you visit a medical doctor and tell him what a pharmacy clerk thinks about your symptoms, the doctor would view it as a waste of time. If a police detective was conducting an investigation, he would want to hear only the facts. (Sometimes I ask customers to think of me as a plumbing detective) I rarely encounter this time-wasting, aggravating problem with customers that know me, but I often experience this problem with new ones. It makes matters even worse when people think they are right, and I am wrong to question their speculation by asking questions. This situation is difficult to describe, but I think most of the aggravation is caused by the feeling that the customer seems to think the plumber is an idiot who needs advice from any source available.

Do tell the plumber about all the plumbing problems you hope to solve on his visit.

Don't wait until the plumber gets to your house before you tell him about additional problems.

Explanation: Most good, trustworthy plumbers try to schedule their work; usually they have other customers waiting for them. It is difficult to figure how long each job will take, but if people add jobs after the plumber arrives at the house, it is impossible. Most good, trustworthy plumbers know that even simple fix-it jobs can develop time-consuming complications. Telling the plumber your complete list of problems allows him to properly schedule the work.

Finding the best plumber might require more research than you think you have time for, but it is worth it. Talking to neighbors is usually the best way to find the best plumber. I really think that even if you have to go around the neighborhood banging on doors (assuming you live in a safe neighborhood), it is worth it. The plumber with experience in your neighborhood is more likely to have the special parts and special knowledge needed, and is more likely to have developed a reputation. The best source of a recommendation is someone with no motive other than trying to promote a top-quality trustworthy plumber. People who recommend a brother or other relative are more than likely just trying to help their relatives.

The type of information you want is:

1. Properly licensed and insured?

2. Established reputation for honesty and quality work?

3. Reasonable hourly labor rate that is comparable to that of an equally qualified plumber working in your area?

4. What is the plumbing specialty?

5. Years of experience?

6. Is the person who comes to your home to perform the work a journeymen or a master plumber?

Personally, I think that if you can find a plumbing company so small that the master plumber who owns the business will actually do the work or be on every job, you will be far better off. Realistically, you might have to settle for a larger company that has a great reputation. It is important that you keep track of the name of the plumber who performed the work at your house. Hopefully, this will make it possible for you to demand this same person each time you call for service if you were happy with him. If you are unhappy but still want to stick with a highly recommended company, make sure they do not send the same plumber next time.

Once you invest time finding the best plumber available, don't destroy any hope of a good long-term relationship because of communication problems.

At first it might take time for you and the plumber to understand each other. He wants to qualify you as a reasonable customer and you want to qualify him as a reasonable plumber. My information concerning the initial call (allowing him to ask the questions and gather important information reasonably efficiently) should help. Keep in mind that he might want to explain how he does business and whether or not he thinks his services are the best for what you need or seem to expect. You shouldn't jump to any conclusions based on the tone of his voice, how he talks, or what you think is going through his mind. If you have determined that he has a good reputation, his reputation should justify you adjusting to his way of doing business (as long as it seems reasonable to you). I hate to keep saying this, but once again this illustrates the importance of carefully checking out the "expert" before you invest your time. Otherwise, you could be wasting time on a complete idiot or a crook. I think it is important to communicate as clearly as possible before, during, and after plumbing services are provided.

After the plumber arrives at your home and sees the situation, there might be optional ways of dealing with the problem.

If you are dealing with a trustworthy plumber, listen carefully and don't always expect a simple, guaranteed solution. Sometimes honest answers are complicated. While you might feel uncomfortable and unsure of the best course of action to take, this honest approach is in your best interest. Usually, a trustworthy plumber can use percentages to help illustrate levels of certainty.

Example: I got a call concerning strange noises when various faucets were used. After I looked around, checked a few shut-off valves to make sure they were fully open, and checked for other possible problems, I told the customer that I was 88 percent sure the problem was a very old pressure reducer on the water main. I also explained that in my opinion, it would not be cost effective to invest more time testing when I was reasonably sure the problem was the old pressure reducer. (It was old enough to justify replacement.) In some cases this would even be justified for a fairly new pressure reducer. If I replaced the pressure reducer and the noise was still there, some customers might say (unfairly) I provided bad services and that I was a bad plumber. As it turned out, I was a hero, and I solved the problem.

Good communication as decisions are made can assure customers that the plumber is looking out for the customer's best interest. That is not to say that a plumber can discuss every possible option or every possible complication. Unfortunately, unexpected complications can pop-up at any time. Trustworthy plumbers try to focus on cost effective communication. Sometimes explaining too much detail can waste time. Often there are no simple no-risk answers. People should look at plumbing as they look at medical problems. When the best surgeon available explains his opinion concerning the best course of action to take, he doesn't guarantee the best results. Honesty and a qualified expert opinion is what you pay for, and that is all you should expect. Good communication will help you understand how and why decisions are made. When it is reasonably possible, you might be presented optional courses of action.

After plumbing services are provided you might be advised concerning possible ways to avoid future problems. Good communication before, during, and after plumbing services are provided will help build a good long-term plumber-customer relationship.

If Things Seem to Have Gone Wrong

I F A MAJOR mistake seems to have been made, it is important that a fair assessment be made. Often, people rush to judgment unfairly and a good plumber could be lost to that particular customer forever. In a situation where a mistake has truly been made, and you need a return trip to correct something that seems to be clearly the plumber's fault, read the following paragraph carefully.

It is important to be aware that many companies have a firm policy of sending the same plumber back to fix any mistakes he made. I think some companies avoid paying their employee by making him fix his mistakes on his own time. Some companies figure by sending the same plumber back, he can learn from his mistakes. I must say that I think it is in the customer's best interest when dealing with a company without an established good reputation, if a different plumber (hopefully a supervisor) fixes mistakes made by others. It must be said that return trips by the same plumber does assure the business that the problem was his fault, and only the original plumber would know exactly what he did and exactly why he did it. (Doing the right thing properly does not guarantee good results.) Once again this brings up the most important factor—the qualifications and reputation of the plumber. If the plumber is qualified and has a reputation for honesty, I think it is fair for the same plumber to return. It is important to realize that many people unfairly rush judgment and assume the plumber is guilty until proven innocent.

Usually a trustworthy plumber finds it difficult to pass judgment on other plumbers. To judge fairly, a trustworthy plumber needs to know detailed information concerning communication between the customer and the plumber being judged. Options presented, options selected, conditions before the plumber arrived, and other factors are important. Intentions and honesty of the plumber and the customer are also important considerations. Look closely at those that find pleasure in passing judgment.

Less than trustworthy plumbers find it easy to judge the work of others. Establish the honesty and qualifications of judgmental plumbers before placing value on their opinion. Judgmental plumbers should be equally specialized and equally trustworthy if the plumber being judged is to be judged fairly.

In summary:

As it becomes more difficult to find good, trustworthy plumbers, it will become ever more important to respect the plumber's time and your money. Don't waste time asking unnecessary questions based on information from unverified experts. Let the plumber control the information gathering process. **Develop a habit of determining an expert's trustworthiness and qualifications before you invest time.**

I refer to an **honest, properly licensed, and insured local plumber,** as a **trustworthy plumber. The best trustworthy plumber usually specializes in the type of plumbing in need of service.** The best trustworthy plumbing advice (opinion) usually comes from the best trustworthy plumber. If you think of plumbing advice like you think of medical advice, it might be easier to **place the proper amount of value on information you gather.** I specialize in all home plumbing problems (except wells and pipes outside the house). Many trustworthy plumbers specialize in wells and pipes outside the house (AKA dig-up work), and they are the best source of advice concerning that specialty. Piping out a new house, restaurant work, and other commercial type work all should be considered specialties. There are many other plumbing specialties, but I think you have the picture. You can find plumbers that do more than one specialty, but - **most of the time, your best advice will come from a trustworthy plumber that works in one specialty.**

Make sure you understand that a trustworthy plumber's advice is based on his opinion and is **his interpretation based on what he has learned from his research and his experience.** I specialize in home plumbing problems in parts of Fairfax County, Virginia, and I have over thirty-eight years of plumbing experience. **Your final decision** on what to do or not do **should be based on advice provided by a local trustworthy plumber that made observations at your home** and should **be in compliance with all local codes and other regulations.** My advice **might help you communicate and ask the best questions. My advice should never replace the advice of a local trustworthy plumber. Always read and understand all disclaimers.** Trustworthy advice might not always provide desirable results, but I think trustworthy, specialized advice provides the best chance for desirable results.

A checklist to help you search for and communicate with the best plumber

THIS CHECKLIST SHOULD help you build a mutually trustworthy relationship with a trustworthy plumber.

- ☐ Do not assume that all plumbers are trustworthy.

- ☐ Do research and establish trust before you call.

☐ Do research and become a trustworthy customer.

☐ Don't expect the best plumber to be the most convenient.

☐ Learn the best way to communicate.

☐ If something goes wrong, don't rush to judgment.

☐ Be careful when one plumber judges another.

This checklist might seem ridiculous, but please keep in mind that hard-working, trustworthy plumbers fear bad communication and unfair judgment.

CHAPTER 5

The Best Way to Search for the Best Plumbing Products

Complicated details make it difficult to select the best plumbing products

HOPE THAT BY illustrating how complicated it is to select the best available plumbing products; you will see why you need the advice of your local trustworthy plumber.

Durability is one of the most important factors to consider as you search for top-quality plumbing products. Many factors affect over all durability. Some factors to consider:

- Chrome seems to hold up much better than other finishes. Fancy state-of-the art finishes seem to scratch, show abrasions, peel, and show other defects much sooner than chrome. Manufacturers have been making claims about state-of-the-art technology that developed durable finishes, but I haven't seen a finish as durable as chrome.

- It takes many years of use, before plumbing products can establish a proven record of reliability and durability. New exciting products often take many years to perfect. When selecting newly developed products, always be aware of the risk. Most old washer-type faucets use to require maintenance about every fifteen years; many people thought washer-less faucets would last forever since there supposedly is no washer to wear out. Many people find that washer-less faucets often need maintenance every eight years or even earlier.

- Many new plumbing products seem to be rushed to market as business focuses more on today's profit and less on long-term profits. Manufacturers and other businesses operate in an overly competitive environment. Most customers expect a bargain and can't tell the difference between durable, top-quality products and products that are only designed to look that way.

Durability and reliability seem to fall in the same category but they are different.

A PLUMBING PRODUCT CAN be reliable under normal use and normal conditions but fail if exposed to abnormal use or abnormal conditions. Many years ago, plumbing products seemed to hold up much better when pushed to the extremes (i.e., spikes in pressure, aggressive water, heavy-handed use, etc.). Manufacturers can blame problems on abnormal use or other conditions, but some products just don't seem to be as durable as others.

After durability and reliability, serviceability and availability of parts should be considered.

Serviceability refers to how difficult it is to replace or install and how difficult is it to repair. Some plumbing products are easy to install if the work is performed while building a new house or installing a new bathroom or installing a new kitchen. Replacing plumbing products often requires working in a very confined area. Some products are very easy to replace and some very difficult. Some products are difficult or not practical to repair (i.e., parts stick together and every trick in the book will not free the parts, time requirements and/or collateral damage prevents cost-effective repairs). Very expensive plumbing products are not necessarily durable, reliable, or serviceable.

Availability of parts is a major concern. Everything eventually wears out (some sooner than others). For many years plumbers found it relatively easy to keep necessary parts on their truck. An assortment of faucet seats, washers, o rings, and other seals made it possible to fix just about anything. Today, manufacturers change products every week and make it impossible to keep all the necessary parts. Cartridges and other parts are often extremely expensive, less than reliable, and very difficult to obtain. The best chance most people have of finding parts is if they keep the paperwork that came with the plumbing product. Most faucets come with model numbers and guarantees.

Guarantees (to the original purchaser) often seem to have replaced quality production, reliability, and durability. People seem to feel safe buying anything with a guarantee. People don't seem to realize that most manufacturers' guarantees only cover parts. Labor can be expensive. When there were major changes in toilets, people started noticing guarantees for toilets. Many major improvements did take place in the design of toilets. As expected, some durability problems did result in premature failure of some new parts. I noticed that one manufacturer eventually had to provide a complete flush valve after it realized a replacement rubber seal was too flimsy. I still see some problems occasionally, but it seems that most problems have been addressed.

Many years ago most faucet manufactures started offering "life-time" guarantees (for the original purchaser). About the same time I started noticing "lifetime" guarantees, I noticed an increase in poorly manufactured and poorly designed faucets. It seems that manufacturers decided that people shouldn't complain about poorly designed or poorly made parts as long as replacement parts are available free. (If people keep the right paperwork, they usually can call a toll free number and get help ordering free parts.) Usually shipping is free—if you are not in a hurry.

Labor expenses to replace parts can get to be a problem for the customer. Some people have so many reoccurring problems that they end up replacing the fixture.

In Summary

HEAVY-HANDED USE, EXPOSURE to abnormal conditions, and other factors often seem to cause more problems with certain plumbing products and fewer problems with others. No manufacturer can protect its product from every overly aggressive person or abnormal condition. Some products are dramatically more durable than others. Some products are dramatically more flimsy than others. Serviceability greatly affects labor costs and whether or not plumbing products can be fixed. Often, important paperwork, model numbers, and guarantees are the key to finding special parts. The key to selecting the best available plumbing products is gathering advice from a local trustworthy plumber.

Trustworthy Plumbers Can Help You Search for Trustworthy Products

Some of the Advice I Provide My Customers Concerning Faucets:

- Try to select a faucet that uses easy-to-find cartridges and other parts. Most major, well-known brand names have faucets available that use their well-established cartridges and other parts. Well-established brand name parts have proven durability and reliability.

- Try to be happy with chrome. Toothpaste is abrasive, and keeping faucets clean requires lots of wear on the finish. Hospitals, restaurants, and laboratories use chrome because it is the best finish. Old top-quality cars have chrome bumpers because it is the most durable surface. I have seen promotions about state-of-the-art finishes that are supposed to be as good as chrome, but I haven't seen one that makes good on the promise.

- Try to make sure handles are easily removed (e.g., remove cover and unscrew retaining screw or some other easy to do process). There are so many different ways to attach handles that most plumbers gave up trying to keep track of all of them. I have seen some where the bottom must be turned clockwise while the top is turned counterclockwise. Some of these handles get jammed because of toothpaste or cleaning products and must be cut out. Many handle designers have found ways to hide the secret combination required for handle removal. I have even seen some handles that require heavy, steady pulling to remove them. (The problem is, if you do this on the wrong faucet, you will break the handle.) Some handles can be removed only if the instructions are readily available (i.e., part A must be turned at three o'clock while part B is turned at twelve o'clock, and then insert an Allen wrench through hole C). If you buy a faucet, always make sure you keep all the papers and instructions. Many of the new style faucets use flimsy plastic parts to attach handles; these parts are easy to break, but it is often difficult to find replacement parts.

- I often find well-established manufacturers that start making very poorly designed new products. When people ask me to recommend plumbing products, I use this knowledge to make suggestions. For example, large handles that control a cartridge that is relying on a small flimsy copper clip is not a durable design. I have fixed faucets after the clip fell off. When a major manufacturer has a very reliable direct connection to a cartridge on some models but decides to add flimsy complicated plastic parts just to provide a little swivel action on other models, I recommend avoiding that particular model. (I've been called to fix those, too.) When I see poorly designed spouts that bleed water or have poorly made plastic bushings at the base, I tell my customers to avoid these models.

I provide details when I talk to my customers. I am afraid to mention manufacturers or models here. Your local trustworthy plumber should be able to provide detailed recommendations when you talk to him and ask him his opinion.

A Checklist to Help You Search for the Best Plumbing Products

THIS CHECKLIST SHOULD help you consider important details. Focus on:

- ❑ Durability

- ❑ Reliability

☐ Serviceability

☐ Availability of parts

Your local trustworthy plumber should help you select the best available products.

CHAPTER 6

Questions and Answers that Explain, Clarify, and I Hope Convince

Questions and Answers

Q. What do you think is the most important thing I should do as I search for advice?

A. Focus on the reputation for **honesty** and focus on **the qualifications of the expert** providing the advice. You can save lots of time and avoid confusion if you **verify the expert before you invest time.**

Q. What's wrong with learning from television?

A. Most how-to television shows are **good entertainment but less than reliable at providing trustworthy information.** I often see **oversimplified** and **misleading** instructions and advice. Sometimes I see **incorrect instructions** and **very rarely** do I **see proper testing procedures.**

Q. Why do you think so many perfectly produced television shows provide misleading and oversimplified plumbing information?

A. It seems that producers control the shows' subject matter and content. Most of the time, it seems that they consult the wrong plumber or other source for technical advice. Producers, like most other people, seem to think all plumbers are equally qualified in every type of plumbing. Most producers haven't worked on plumbing and do not realize how important details are. Most producers are not aware of the problems misleading, oversimplified, and sometimes incorrect, instructions cause.

Even when a trustworthy specialized expert is consulted, details can be left out; often, too much can be squeezed into a half-hour show. A typical half hour show (controlled by a producer) would show how to replace a toilet. If a trustworthy plumber controlled the content, a half-hour show might properly illustrate how to remove a toilet. It would require an additional half hour show to properly illustrate installing a toilet. [Note: I wrote a script that included a reasonable amount of complications that frequently occur when removing a toilet. After including a reasonable amount of details, I determined that it would require a half-hour show to properly illustrate these important details.]

Q. Why do you think it would take a half-hour show to show people how to remove a toilet? Wouldn't that be a boring show?

A. Based on my experience, people need to see important details. Often, people create major problems when they learn just enough information to get in trouble. If a show (based on trustworthy expert advice) carefully explained the most frequent complications (and the solutions), it would take at least a half hour to show people how to remove a toilet. To address frequently occurring complications and how to deal with them requires important, frequently overlooked instructional details. The script I wrote illustrates major mistakes that might even seem funny, as long as it doesn't happen in your home. Silly things like a pencil falling out of a shirt pocket and down an open pipe, a flood from a shut-off valve that almost works correctly, or a broken toilet because of an aggravating nut that will not unscrew. (My script shows people how to carefully cut out a nut when it will not unscrew.) Top-quality information doesn't have to be boring, but it must be focused on the best interest of the viewers.

Q. Often, I get conflicting advice that leaves me feeling confused and overwhelmed. How do I determine which "expert" to believe?

A. Before investing your time getting advice, check the qualifications of the expert. Make sure the advice is coming from a real expert. Also, try to determine if the expert is providing honest advice or just trying to sell something. Don't waste time getting advice from questionable advisers. Value advice according to the amount of trust you have in the expert. If you think the experts you have consulted are equally **honest,** place more value on the one that has the most **specialized qualifications.**

Q. Nonprofit consumer organizations seem to have a good reputation and seem to use experts to provide advice; do you consider those organizations a good source of expert plumbing advice?

A. In my opinion no one is perfect. I try to carefully monitor available sources of plumbing advice and in my opinion the nonprofit organizations I monitored need to take plumbing more seriously. When I try to place a value on an "expert opinion," I focus on the expert that provides the opinion (advice). The organizations I researched seemed to have qualified experts advising them on automobiles, appliances, and other topics, but I haven't found one using a truly qualified plumbing expert. Also, I have noticed major mistakes in the plumbing advice category.

Q. Could you provide an example of what you think was a major mistake in plumbing advice provided by a nonprofit consumer organization?

A. Sure. One of the best-known consumer organizations did a section on chemical drain cleaners. I agreed with their advice concerning chemical drain cleaners (after a drain is completely stopped up don't try it) but was shocked when they went on to recommend using boiling water to unstop a drain. Dumping boiling hot water down a drain is extremely bad advice—in my opinion that isn't even debatable. That bad advice and other bad plumbing advice convinced me they are consulting the wrong experts. They need to consult the best plumbers that specialize in **plumbing problems in the home**.

Q. Why do you consider dumping boiling water down a drain bad advice?

A. Boiling water damages plumber's putty, rubber, plastic connections, and other plumbing parts. Boiling water often greatly shortens the life of a garbage disposer because it damages the rubber seals. Boiling water can easily crack a bathroom sink. Boiling hot water can cause a bathtub drain or other drain to leak. I fix these problems and others. I see the results of melted plastic parts, cracked washers, and other problems. There are other problems it can cause, but I think I have listed enough.

Q. If boiling water is so bad, why doesn't it cause problems when people dump pasta over the sink?

A. It does. Most people don't notice it, but eventually, boiling water will cause problems. I ask my customers to run plenty of cold water and pour boiling water slowly when straining pasta. I always recommend that people protect the sink from boiling hot water by running plenty of cold water or by catching the water in another pan so it can cool down before it is poured down the drain.

Q. If boiling water is so bad, do people need to worry about the hot water from their faucet or dishwasher?

A. No. That water is usually not hot enough to hurt anything (usually 140 degrees or less). The highest setting I have ever seen on a residential water heater is 170 degrees and even that does not seem to cause any problems with the plumbing. Keep in mind that there are hot-water dispensers that produce 192 degree or hotter water. People with those dispensers need to cool the water down before it is allowed down the drain. Any water hotter than 170 degrees should be cooled before allowing it down the drain.

Q. Are there things that people can do that might unclog a drain?

A. Hot water, as long as it is 140 degrees or less might help but don't try it in a toilet. It is always a good idea to avoid a sudden change of temperature in any fixture. Hot water in a toilet can crack the toilet and/or melt the wax seal.

A plunger might help unclog a sink or bathtub. Any overflow holes must be covered with a wet rag, and you should use the plunger to try to pull the blockage back and not push it down. Check for leaks after you finish. Often the immediate area can be cleaned with a toothbrush or one of the new zip-type cleaning strips that can be purchased for less than three dollars. Hand snakes will often work for a bathroom sink, a shower, or a bathtub if used carefully. Chemicals or high-pressure cans are not worth the risk. A special snake for toilets (AKA a closet auger) is good to have around in case of a toilet stoppage. If you buy a closet auger, get the clerk to show you how to use it. Sometimes a plunger designed for toilets will work on toilets. Always try to pull back the problem causing the stoppage. Pushing a comb, toothbrush, or other object down from a toilet to a drain pipe is risky. Sewer stoppages are much worse than toilet stoppages.

Q. Are there things that people can do to help avoid a stoppage?

A. To help avoid stoppages:

- Learn, the proper way to use a garbage disposer.

- Avoid putting large amounts of garbage in the disposer.

- Wipe off dishes into a container for a compost pile or trash container before placing them in the dishwasher.

- Wipe pans before washing them.

- Avoid grease going down the drain.

- Be careful what is flushed in toilets.

- Don't overload a toilet

- Read the toilet section of this book

- Try to keep a hair catching strainer on bathtubs

- When a bar of soap gets small enough to wash down the drain, throw it in the trash or combine small pieces into one large bar. Soap can stop up a drain. Also, soap can stick to hair and cause a build up.

- If your clothes washer dumps into a laundry sink, carefully attach a lint filter.

Filling the sink or bathtub with water that is 140 degrees or less and letting it drain can help keep the drain clean and sometimes improve a slow drain. (In rare cases this could also cause a complete stoppage.) Don't store small items close to a plumbing fixture where they might fall into the fixture. Children should never be allowed to store toys in a bathroom. Small children should never be left unattended in the bathroom.

Q. Do you consider it dangerous to use chemical drain cleaners?

A. Yes. I consider it more dangerous than cutting food with a knife. People understand that a knife is dangerous, and because of that, they are more likely to use a knife properly and carefully.

Most people don't seem to understand how dangerous chemicals are. Chemicals are often used improperly and carelessly. Chemical drain cleaners can cause serious bodily injury (especially to the eyes).

I have seen major plumbing damage resulting from careless misuse of chemicals. I tell my customers to not use chemical drain cleaners. It seems to me that my hot (not boiling) water treatment before a complete clog is much safer and probably equally beneficial.

For those people who are determined to use a chemical drain cleaner, I provide some advice. Follow the directions carefully; multiple overdoses or using multiple bottles at one time can create an extremely dangerous situation. I have seen extremely expensive damage from reckless use of chemical drain cleaners. Bodily damage is a real concern, especially if you get the chemicals in your eyes. If there is any chance that any trace of a chemical drain cleaner will sit in standing water, I strongly recommend against its use. If people wait until the drain is completely stopped up (water stays in the fixture for more than a minute longer than normal), I think it is too late to safely attempt any chemical drain cleaner. Even if you don't consider the danger, it is more likely to make the blockage more difficult to clear.

Q. There are many conflicting opinions concerning the proper use of a garbage disposer, can you provide some advice concerning garbage disposers?

A. When possible put garbage in a compost pile or in a trash can. Even with the best garbage disposer, problems can develop when large amounts of garbage go down the drain.

When you have to put garbage in a garbage disposer, the way you do it is more important than the quality of the disposer. I did a survey for three years, and I asked people how they run garbage through their disposer. The people in my survey were people that had called me because of a stopped-up sink. About ninety percent of these people scraped their plates, turned on the water, and then turned on the disposer. Many of these people experienced yearly or more frequent, stoppages. After I asked these people to start slowly feeding garbage while the water and the disposer are running, they rarely experience a stoppage. Also, they avoid a stinky disposer and avoid problems with a stopped-up line from the dishwasher.

The practice of putting garbage in the disposer (AKA batch feeding) before the disposer and water are on, is not what I call the proper use of the disposer. Some disposers can only be used by batch feeding, and if children or mentally challenged people are in the household, I think the trade off is worth it.

Q. Why do you indicate that your advice is provided to improve communication between the customer and the plumber? Is it not provided to help do it yourselfers?

A. I suspect that do it yourselfers, tile men, carpenters, floor install-ers, and others will use my detailed advice to improve their chances of doing plumbing correctly, but that is not the intended purpose of my advice. More money (and inconvenience) can be saved by properly communicating with an honest, qualified plumber than by doing it yourself. Do it yourselfers often create more problems than they solve. The gamble of long-term risk (future flooding or worse) is too great. Licensed, qualified, and insured plumbers should do your plumbing. I think the best place to gamble is Las Vegas.

Q. If the local plumbing code is a minimum standard, why should I focus so much on the local code?

A. **Always make sure you comply with all governing regula-tions and codes**. These regulations and codes supersede any advice I provide or advice anyone else provides. Weather, geological factors, and other conditions vary. If there is any doubt, always check with the proper local governing regulators. Locally authorized governing officials should be able to advise you if any variation from the code is better than the minimum standard.

Q. I can get plenty of free advice, what do you think is wrong with doing research that way?

A. You can spend hours searching for **trustworthy plumbing advice** and most likely you will end up misled or more confused than when you started. I often monitor available **free** plumbing informa-tion and have found that most of it is very well produced, but **has less than trustworthy content**. Selecting valuable information from the tremendous amount of **free junk plumbing information** is extremely difficult. Many Web sites seem to focus on advertising revenue generated by clicks or other means. Many of these sites seem to provide incorrect or over simplified answers to complicated questions. Dishonest advice can be used to sell products, attract interest, and falsely project an image of a "real expert." Usually if you ever find trustworthy advice, it will either be a sample of information you can purchase, or, it is provided to sell products. Free advice can only be considered free if you place no value on your time. Free advice can only be valuable if you can establish the trustworthiness of the expert.

Q. What message do you think is most important?

A. **Details** are important. Details concerning:

- Who you trust for advice.

- Who you trust to do plumbing in your home.

- The plumbing products installed in your home.

- How your plumbing is maintained.

Q. I don't think I have a frost-proof outside faucet, so I turned off my outside faucet using the valve inside my house. Then I opened the outside faucet to drain it. After the freezing weather was over, I turned on the inside valve and found water spraying inside the wall. What do you think happened?

A. First of all, if you had a frost-proof outside faucet (a faucet with a stem long enough to stop the water inside where it is safe from freezing), usually you would only have to make sure you disconnect the hose and anything else you have connected to it. That is supposed to allow the exposed section of the outside faucet to drain.

Some people are not sure if they have a frost-proof outside faucet, so I tell them that if they have an inside shut-off valve for their outside faucet, they should assume the outside faucet is not frost-proof.

Most of the people I talk to don't winterize the outside faucet properly. When a pipe freezes and breaks, it is usually because some one failed to do an important step in the winterization process. The proper steps are:

1. Turn off the inside valve that shuts off the water to the outside faucet.

2. After disconnecting the hose, open the outside faucet. If there is a vacuum breaker or any other device attached to the outside faucet, make sure you open it. Otherwise, there is a good chance that it will not allow proper draining.

3. While the outside faucet is opened, unscrew the small cap attached to the side of the inside shut-off valve. [Caution: I have seen some inside shut-off valves that were installed backward; if the small cap continues to spray forcibly, the valve was probably incorrectly installed]. If you find that the inside shut-off valve is incorrectly installed, quickly tighten the cap back in place. If the inside shut-off valve does not have a small cap or if it is improperly installed, a plumber will have to correct the problem. Some times, the rubber seal inside the cap will stick, so you might have to carefully peel it off. Water might spray, squirt, or drip from this cap. If the inside shut off is higher than the outside faucet, you might hear it suck air.

I try to explain to people that if they fail to open the little cap, the water in the pipe usually will not drain out because air is needed to break the vacuum and allow the water to drain out. Unless you do all three steps, and make sure that water drains out, water will most likely still be in the pipe and faucet in the cold wall. Any water left behind will usually freeze and make it possible to split the pipe and/or the outside faucet.

Q. Why is it often difficult to get a fixed price or an estimate for small plumbing jobs?

A. Trustworthy plumbers usually realize that complications can pop up at any time. Even after looking at the proposed work, fixed prices and estimates are almost impossible to provide for small plumbing jobs. Since it is almost impossible to explain every possible complication, it is almost impossible to provide a set price for small plumbing jobs. Pricing for a new bathroom or other large job is more practical and worthwhile. Large jobs have enough potential profit to make extensive communication cost effective but small jobs don't. Plumbers can spend more time talking about work than the work would actually take. Small plumbing jobs expose the plumber to many possible complications that are not practical to predict. As I mentioned earlier, free estimates aren't really free; their cost is built into every estimate, so one way or the other, customers pay for what they get.

Consumer agencies and others seem to think that a good plumber should be able to look at small plumbing jobs and provide a fixed price or at least an estimate. These people seem to be making a big mistake. By focusing on ways they think competition will keep prices honest, they shift the advantage to less-than-honest plumbers.

Many customers fail to realize that when they agree to an outrageous price, they make that price legitimate. When a customer requests an estimate for a small job, many plumbers will double the price (or more than double the price). If doubling the price really protects the customer from unexpected expenses, the added expense might be justifiable; it could be considered "extra" insurance or insurance against "extra charges." If this process truly guaranteed that any possible complications would be taken care of at no additional expense, there would be a clear understanding of what customers were paying for. Like most insurance policies, lots of fine print is necessary to indicate what is covered and what is not. In the absence of clearly defined terms, the customer only gets as much protection as the plumber chooses to allow. When customers agree to extremely high prices before work begins they usually lose the right to a legitimate complaint.

The customer might not be concerned about unnecessary extra charges if the extra charges really provided protection. If the customer agrees to an outrageous price because he doesn't want to take off another day of work or thinks he is buying insurance against extra expenses or some other reason, he doesn't seem to have a legitimate complaint. Competitive biding for big jobs might require a built in 10 percent mark up to protect against unforeseeable extra work. Competitive biding for small jobs often requires a 100 percent mark up to protect against a limited amount of unforeseeable extra work.

Most trustworthy plumbers don't like to bid on small jobs for this reason. Most -less than-trustworthy plumbers enjoy big profits by using this type of pricing.

People shop for cheap prices as they fail to realize prices can always change. Complications can always develop. The skill and honesty of the plumber is important. What looks like a bargain might just be a bait and switch or a get in the door price. What is most disturbing is how this belief that all plumbers are the same has lowered the quality of plumbing.

Competition for small plumbing jobs could help consumers if all plumbers were the same. If all plumbers were equally honest, and they all provided the same quality of work, comparing prices would be easy.

Bargain shopping seems to have resulted in most shoppers losing sight of what hiring a plumber or other tradesmen is all about; **you are supposed to be paying a reasonable fee for the services of a qualified expert.** These days most people don't know the qualifications of the plumber. People don't know if he is cutting corners or playing other tricks on them. The wheeling-dealing dishonest plumber or other tradesmen often makes more money than the honest highly qualified one.

Meanwhile, people wonder why homes are built poorly and plumbers and other tradesmen don't do work like they use to. Doing plumbing over thirty-eight years, I have noticed that many of the best tile men, house painters, carpenters, plumbers, and others have been forced out of business by unfair bargain shopping. **If people really want to gain the greatest amount of control when they hire a plumber or other tradesman, they must search for the best. Keep track of the time a trustworthy plumber works to solve plumbing problems and pay a fair price for his time. If you pay for a less than trustworthy plumber, it might be a long time before you realize what a huge mistake you made.**

CHAPTER 7

Small Jobs, Competition, and the Real World

Shop Cost Effectively
How much does it cost to replace a toilet?

IF THERE WERE only a few possible complications to worry about, an estimate to replace a toilet could include the worst-case scenario (at the risk of providing an outrageous price). Because there are so many possible complications (most are rare), and trustworthy plumbers don't want to mislead customers, many trustworthy plumbers do not try to estimate the cost to replace a toilet or do other small plumbing jobs.

Some plumbers provide a price for the work if there are no complications. The problem with that is if major complications develop, many customers will end up very unhappy (most people expect no more than a 10 percent increase in the price).

Most toilets have two nuts that attach the toilet to the floor (some have four). Looking at these nuts does not always provide a true estimate of how much it will cost to remove them (time is money). If each nut unscrews normally, it might take less than ten seconds. If the whole bolt turns it might take fifteen minutes or more to remove each nut (the nut might have to be cut out).

If it is discovered that the flange is broken it will take even more time to fix or replace it. Nut removal problems and broken flange problems are only two possible complications that require extra time to fix. Shut-off valve problems are a frequently occurring complication that requires additional cost.

Most people realize that after a shut-off valve is turned off, a properly working valve will shut off 100 percent. What most people don't realize is that often problems with a shut-off valve only show up after the valve is turned back on. A small drip close to the handle from the stem seal (AKA packing nut) can result in repair or replacement of the shut-off valve. The remedy for this problem can be very simple, very complicated, or anywhere in between. I hope my explanation of how to fix this problem will illustrate why it is almost impossible to know all these variables ahead of time.

Sometimes, turning the packing nut (the nut close to the handle) will stop a drip from a leaky stem seal. The only way to tell is tighten the packing nut and test it for at least ten minutes (clean up or other work can be done while testing). If the stem seal continues to leak, usually water to the whole house will have to be turned off so the leaky shut-off valve can be repaired or replaced. Once again, this additional work will cost money and expose the homeowner to even more possible complications, including:

- The main shut-off valve might not shut off 100 percent.

- The main shut-off valve stem seal might drip after it is turned back on.

- Draining and refilling the system might aggravate a defect in the system and cause other complications (even when drained and refilled properly).

- Draining and refilling the system might stir up sediment and/ or cause other problems (even when drained and refilled properly).

- Disturbing pipes might aggravate a defect in the system and cause other complications (even when work is done carefully and properly).

As you see the various complications, I hope you can understand all the possible combinations of costly extra work. There are too many variables to put a price on.

Some complications that often require extra cost when replacing a toilet include:

- Rusty bolts that hold the toilet bowl to the floor (AKA closet bolts) have to be cut out.

- The shut-off valve to the toilet fails to turn off 100 percent or leaks after all the work is completed and has to be replaced.

- The flange that bolts to the bottom of the toilet (AKA closet flange) is too low or too high, and adjusting the amount of wax will not correct the problem properly.

- Floor imperfections make it necessary to do lots of shimming to prevent wobble and hold the toilet reasonably level.

- Broken, cracked, or other defects in the closet flange or pipe.

I could go on and on about frequently occurring complications that cost money to fix. By now I hope you can see why many trustworthy plumbers do not provide estimates or a set price for small plumbing repairs and replacements. By now I hope you can understand why you need to find a trustworthy plumber.

A trustworthy plumber will work carefully and try to avoid as many complications as possible. It is important to realize that complications can always occur, but your best chance of avoiding complications is by finding the best plumber.

If you still need convincing, please read more about this topic.

Why Trustworthy Plumbers Don't Like to Bid on Small Jobs

PEOPLE OFTEN CALL requesting the price to replace a wax ring under a toilet. I try to explain that I don't have a set price for small jobs like this. I have invested lots of time trying to explain to customers that guessing at a fair price to do small jobs is usually a waste of time. Attempting to explain important details and attempting to make sure each customer understands these details is not cost effective.

Some consumer magazines recommend that people try to get a set price for all plumbing work. Some publishers seem to think that creating competition is always in the consumer's best interest. I think expecting set prices (AKA estimates) for a small plumbing job is a big mistake.

Competition must take place on a level playing field to be of any benefit. Only when equally honest and equally qualified plumbers compete for exactly the same work is there a level playing field. Consumers often pay high prices for low-quality work because most trustworthy plumbers avoid competition that places them on an uneven playing field.

Trustworthy plumbers don't want to mislead people. Guessing at competitive prices for small jobs can easily provide prices that are outrageously high or unrealistically low. Less than trustworthy plumbers can make big profits by providing high prices that can still increase if complications develop. Most trustworthy plumbers want to make an honest living being paid a fair price for work they do—no more, no less.

I have known a few trustworthy plumbers that would make an educated guess at the necessary labor for a small job (assuming no complications). These plumbers usually figure the labor and double it to provide an estimate. This type of estimate would include some complications (up to a 100 percent increase), but not all possible complications (rarely-but-possible complications could result in more than a 100 percent increase). If the work was completed with no complications, the plumber gets paid twice as much as he normally would and risks damaging his good reputation (if the customer feels like they paid too much). If a major complication requires a significant amount of extra labor (more than a 100 percent amount of extra expense), the customer is required to pay for it. If customers don't fully understand the limitations of a fixed price or an estimated price, trustworthy plumbers risk unfair damage to their reputation.

In a perfect world where all plumbers and all customers are honest, competitive biding for small plumbing jobs might be effective. In a perfect world, all parties would fully understand the gambling aspects and an estimate or set price could be truly competitive. Sadly, we don't live in a perfect world. Competition is not the key to fair pricing, and competition will not make a dishonest plumber honest. I have a three-step process that will provide your best chance of paying a fair price for small plumbing jobs. This process can also help you to determine if you paid too much after trusting a plumber.

The Three most important steps required to get the best plumbing work at the best price.

1. Determine the qualifications and honesty of the plumber before he does the work (check his reputation and qualifications).

2. Compare his hourly labor rate with other equally qualified plumbers in your area.

3. Keep track of the amount of time he works at your home.

Those three steps are also important with large contracted plumbing jobs. It might be more difficult to keep track of the amount of hours spent working at your home, but it is worth the effort.

When presented a contract, you should ask how many man hours (hours a qualified plumber works at your home) are figured in the price. After the work is completed, you can compare the estimated man hours to the actual man hours the job took. This helps you get a rough idea of whether or not you got your money's worth. After the contract work is completed, it is a good sign if the work took the expected amount of man hours. As long as there isn't a big difference between the amount of man hours estimated and the amount of man hours it took, there is probably no reason for concern.

Some people think that keeping track of man hours is a waste of time. Some think that dishonest plumbers will just work slower or find other ways to cheat. I disagree with these people. Talking to many people, I have learned that more than 90 percent of the people who felt cheated complained that after agreeing to a high price, they realized that they didn't know the qualifications of the worker and didn't realize the high price only provided a small amount of labor. Keeping track of man hours is important because it will provide a hint of whether or not details were left out. If you fail to keep track of man hours, you will have no idea what you paid for.

CHAPTER 8

Uneven Playing Fields

Uneven Playing Fields Create Big Problems for Consumers and Professionals

THIS STORY HELPS illustrate the uneven playing field that honest, highly qualified professionals often find themselves on.

The House Painter

TALKING TO TOP-QUALITY house painters, tile men, carpenters, and others I shall refer to as trustworthy contractors, I noticed a common problem that also relates to top-quality plumbing. Competitive shopping often places honest, highly qualified professionals on an uneven playing field with dishonest, low-quality professionals. Important details necessary for the best long-term results require extra work that is figured in by trustworthy contractors but not by others. This is the biggest problem that creates an uneven playing field.

Prices, promises, and guarantees are only valuable if they come from a trustworthy contractor. Dishonest contractors can offer anything the customer wants. Most people don't seem to understand this, and they expect trustworthy contractors to offer the same prices, promises, and guarantees. This is the second biggest problem that creates an uneven playing field.

The story about the trustworthy house painter is a good way to illustrate the decline in quality work provided at a fair price. The most recent trend created a business environment where promises seem to replace quality work. Many years ago, people often paid low prices for low-quality work provided by less-than-honest professionals. The recent trend often results in higher-than-necessary prices for low-quality work.

I talked to a house painter and learned that preparing a house for paint is often more work than the actual painting. Scraping, cleaning, caulking, and priming take time. When a trustworthy painter figures a price to paint the outside of a house, he might figure one day to scrape out old caulking and loose paint. One day to caulk and prime, and one day to paint. Three days of work by a qualified trustworthy painter use to cost about $1,000.00 (including labor, paint, and other material). An honest, trustworthy painter gives a price of $1,000.00 and spends three days providing a top-quality paint job that will probably last at least ten years.

I have heard stories of people getting bids on a paint job, and the prices came in at $700.00 to $1,000.00. Often the people go with the cheapest price. After the cheap paint job, they realize that the complete job was done in one day. They paid $700.00 for a questionable painter to work one day. The trustworthy highly qualified painter would have worked hard for three days. These people did not get a bargain paint job. Even if the bargain painter provided a guarantee for one or two years, the paint job is not likely to last very long. The bargain painters get plenty of work as bargain shoppers think they can outsmart the professionals.

Times are rapidly changing. When I first wrote the House Painter story, I just wrote it like I use to tell it to my customers, now I realize that this story needs to be updated.

Years of customers shopping for the best price have evolved, now it seems that slick-talking salesmen often talk people into overly high priced contracts and if you agree to pay the price, you can't complain. Slick talking promises have replaced low prices.

Using the right sales pitch and making every effort to accommodate potential customers by providing "free" estimates, house painters and other contractors provide high-priced contracts for low-quality services. By letting the customer hear what they want to hear and meeting them at any time of day or night, these contractors make lots of money. The best house painters, tile men, carpenters, and plumbers often go unappreciated, and while I must say most plumbers survive, often the others go out of business.

Businesses that tell customers what ever they want to hear make big profits, one year or more guarantees, promises of lowest price, artificial discounts, anything that makes the customer feel like they are in complete control. Later, people begin to realize that in the real world, bargains are found when you find the best house painter, plumber, or other craftsman, and you pay a fair price for his services (no more, no less).

Most estimates and contract prices have provisions for extra charges if complications develop. Customers might think they are getting a set price when they are not. A fair price is when you are charged a fair price for the time a qualified craftsman spends providing services. If a contractor provides a price, after the job is finished, you should consider how much time a qualified craftsmen spent on your project.

When you pay for services the three most important factors are:

1. Honesty

2. Qualifications (including proper license and insurance)

3. Time spent working

An honest professional will provide:

- Honest details concerning his qualifications and experience.

- A fair labor rate for a person with his qualifications.

- Honest answers, promises, and guarantees.

- Services that are focused on your best long-term interest.

- Labor charges that reflect the actual amount of time required to solve your problem.

Estimates or so-called set prices can change. Details often make the difference between long-term solutions and short term solutions. Focus on finding trustworthy contractors, and you will be glad you did.

CHAPTER 9

Entertainment versus Research

Is It Entertainment or Worthwhile Research?

WE LIVE IN a society that seems to place too much trust in the entertainment industry. People often watch how-to television shows thinking they can gather enough information to do it themselves. Later, after they realize that they started to do something that is beyond their capabilities, people often wish they had spent their research time more wisely. People are beginning to realize that entertainment is usually controlled by entertainment experts not plumbing experts. Remember the example of the how to install a toilet show I mentioned earlier? It illustrates that when the focus is on entertainment, often, important details are rushed through or skipped entirely.

Including all necessary information and the frequent complications and mistakes could be done in an honest and entertaining way. Some complications and mistakes seem amusing, as long as it doesn't happen to you. Most people who have experienced unexpected complications and mistakes would appreciate added details.

People are beginning to expect more details and better content. **Better content requires better use of the best experts**. The best experts can provide the proper details and the proper amount of details.

Only highly experienced **plumbers that specialize in home plumbing problems know the most frequent complications**, mistakes, and solutions. Producers will soon learn to appreciate the value and necessity of these experts. People who like to do things themselves will see the difference between only entertainment type shows and truly valuable programs. Armed with the right information, people will deal effectively with complications and will make fewer mistakes.

As people enjoy the benefits of trustworthy content, the Internet, and other media will be forced to focus on better content. As technology makes quality production easier it also makes quality content more difficult to find. Finding a trustworthy source of top-quality expert advice is difficult. To avoid big mistakes that come from trusting bad advice, smart people are beginning to expect producers to reveal the qualifications of experts providing technical advice.

Technical advice has more than one layer. Experts are not just needed for technical advice. Experts are needed to provide guidance for the overall production. When the overall production is misleading or in other ways oversimplified- honest, qualified experts can help correct the problem.

In summary:

My opinion is that in the past and presently, most media productions concerning plumbing have major problems. Productions often contain oversimplified, misleading and sometimes incorrect information. It seems that producers often rely on the wrong experts or don't seem to make the proper use of experts. The experts providing advice (AKA opinions) should always be identified. As trustworthy experts begin to provide much needed guidance, producers will greatly improve content.

A Newfound Respect for Honest, Specialized Plumbers

SOON, A NEW trend will set the stage for a new way of dealing with plumbers. Quality plumbing provides the necessary sanitation that prevents health problems. As people focus on avoiding health problems, they will learn to understand the importance of durable, reliable plumbing.

Durability and reliability will improve as people learn to focus on important details. Details concerning plumbing products, details concerning how they are installed, and details concerning how plumbing is maintained make the services of an honest, specialized, plumber essential. Mold, reoccurring problems, health issues, and a focus on long-term results will change the way people think of plumbers. As people begin to realize that the plumber protects the health of the nation, a newfound respect for plumbers will develop.

Soon, product developers will realize that durable, reliable plumbing products require better design and better testing. Manufacturers will begin to realize how poor design and poor manufacturing drains profits. Profits can easily disappear as customers call to complain. Lifetime guarantees often shift last year's profits to this year's loss and future losses. Expensive telephone operators, shipping, handling, and other necessary costs of lifetime guarantees can make tracking profits impossible. Soon, as recalls and class action lawsuits develop, manufactures will be forced to improve design and production. Products will then improve. Specialized plumbers will help manufacturers understand how important often overlooked details are. Products will improve as manufacturers make specialized plumbers a key part of the design process.

As people realize that they can use the same skills they use when searching for the best medical doctor to search for the best plumber, they will. As people learn to focus on seeking the plumber that specializes in the type of plumbing services they need, they will. As people search for specialized plumbers they can trust, they will place the proper amount of value on specialized plumbers that earned a good reputation. This new trend will greatly improve sanitation in the home.

Why Is It Not Possible to Make a Dishonest Plumber Honest?

FIRST, I MUST say that I think most plumbers are honest. All people should be given the benefit of the doubt. There should never be a rush to judgment. The current trend seems to be guilty until proven innocent, and that is not fair. The current trend seems to favor expensive, wasteful business practices, and it is not necessarily dishonest to pass these added expenses on to the customer.

Honest business people that are forced to play wasteful competitive bargain shopping games for small jobs can justify charging higher fees. Higher prices are required to cover free estimates, risk, image building, and other expenses. These higher prices are not necessarily dishonest prices. Large plumbing businesses that try to give the customers what they want when they need it are often forced to hire less-qualified plumbers. Giving the customers what they want when they need it is expensive and often lowers the quality of the people available to do the work. So, people who prefer "free" estimates, convenience, and other "satisfy the customer" treatment should not always consider high prices for low-quality work dishonest.

Now, I will provide tricks that dishonest plumbers could play.

1. Cutting corners. Often, I hear stories about outrageously high prices for plumbing work that only took two hours or less. Most of these people got an estimate (AKA a price for the work). Most thought the estimate was outrageously high. Since they already had a plumber there and didn't want to take off work again, they agreed to the amount. Frequently, estimating is based on the amount of time an "estimating book" allows for the plumbing work. Estimate prices are based on the amount of time normally required to properly perform the work by a qualified plumber. The best of these books provide prices based on including important, time-consuming details. Cut corners (rush through or skip details) and lots of money can be made. A four-hour job should take four hours. When a customer pays for four hours, he should be very concerned if the work only took two hours. When a customer gets two hours of work for a job that should take four hours, being cheated out of money should not be the primary concern. The most important concern should be the quality of the work. Long-term results are directly affected by the quality of the work. Quality work requires careful focus on important details. For example, toilets that move a little will cause big problems over time, even if the movement might not even be obvious until long after the plumber leaves. Leaking might not be obvious until long after he's left.

2. Smoke-and-mirror prices. Prices can always change. What is included in the price can be difficult to define. It is easy to present a dishonest image of what the customer is paying for. Examples include get-in-the-door prices, selling promises and guarantees, and selling convenience.

3. Overlooking complications. If complications might be considered an included element of the estimated work

(deliberately overlook it). If it appears a complication might provide future money-making opportunities, deliberately over look it. For example, a small leak on a shut-off valve that isn't fixed when noticed will mean a larger job later.

4. Fine print. Present what the customer wants to hear clearly. Put important details that customers don't want, in fine print. Here's a tip: the world use to run on trust and a handshake, now the world runs on fine print—read it!

5. Deliberately or carelessly creating complications. Expensive complications can always develop; the frequency of complications will be directly related to the person doing the work. Honest, highly qualified plumbers will try to keep complications to a minimum. Dishonest plumbers can use complications to increase profits or to make excuses for sloppy, careless work. An example would be rushing through the job too fast, inexperience about techniques that avoids unnecessary stress on adjoining connections, or deliberately creating future work.

6. Bonuses and other incentives for workers could create a conflict of interest. Many plumbing companies offer incentives and bonuses for plumbers that replace a disposer, a water heater, a faucet, or other plumbing fixture. I think plumbers should always focus on the customer's best interest. Fixing or replacing decisions should be based on honest recommendations that provide customers with the most cost-effective way to provide the best long-term results. Bonuses and other incentives can easily bribe dishonest plumbers that place personal financial interest in front of the customer's best interest. It would be helpful if customers were made aware of incentive programs. Customers should be aware of the possible influence incentives create.

7. Other dishonest tricks that are often unsuspected by the customer. Deliberately oversimplifying, misleading, and providing worthless promises are just a few dishonest tricks that fool customers. There are an unlimited amount of dishonest tricks and new ones are invented everyday.

It is impossible to make dishonest people honest. It seems to me that bargain shopping and expecting a plumber to talk you into trusting him, greatly increases the chances that you will end up with a dishonest plumber. If you think you can trick a plumber into a super bargain price, you make yourself a prime target for a dishonest plumber. Dishonest plumbers love dishonest customers.

Dishonest plumbers like people that expect them to provide a sales pitch. Verbally creating trust is much easier than building and protecting a good reputation. The best way to find a trustworthy plumber is to talk to neighbors and find a qualified plumber with a good reputation. Don't judge a plumber by his ability to accommodate your schedule. Learn to appreciate the difference between plumbers and trustworthy plumbers, and you will enjoy the best possible long-term results.

CHAPTER 10

A Shortage of Specialized Plumbers and What You Can Do

The Secret: There is a Shortage of Specialized Plumbers

PEOPLE SMART ENOUGH to realize that there is a shortage of specialized plumbers will benefit from my advice and be able to greatly increase their chances of finding a trustworthy specialized plumber. If you follow my advice, you should be able to build a mutually trusting relationship with a trustworthy specialized plumber.

My Advice

- Try to find a plumber that specializes in the type of plumbing work you need, i.e., solving problems in the home, pipes outside, remodeling, piping out a new home, commercial plumbing, medical plumbing, and others.

- Check the qualifications of the person that will do the work.

- Check the reputation of the person that will do the work. (Usually talking to neighbors is the best way, but sometimes you can benefit from nonprofit consumer advocate organizations.)

- Find out what the hourly labor rate is.

- Learn to communicate efficiently and effectively (read my section on communication).

- Keep track of the amount of time the plumber works solving your problem or providing other plumbing services.

- Try to avoid recommending your trustworthy specialized plumber to people that do not seem trustworthy.

CHAPTER 11

What You Need to Learn

Learn Important Details: Searching for Leaks

SEARCHING FOR LEAKS can be time consuming. Often, people could save lots of money if they knew how to search for a leak. Sometimes, after searching for a leak, it might be determined that there is not a plumbing leak. Tile, caulking, a careless person not properly closing a shower curtain, or some other problem might have caused what appears to be a plumbing leak.

The Dry Finger Test Can Help You Before and After You Call a Plumber

AS SILLY AS it might seem, details are especially important when testing or searching for a leak. Cold can feel wet. Small streams that provide major leaks can hide in areas that make them difficult to see. Extremely fine squirts that look like a cobweb, small drips, and many other difficult to find leaks can be found using the *dry finger test*. Learning the dry finger test is one of the most important steps to learn before you start searching for leaks. Searching for leaks before and after you call a plumber can save you lots of money, aggravation, and time. More importantly, it should help provide a sanitary living environment for your family.

How to Do the Dry Finger Test

AFTER YOU MAKE sure a finger is completely dry, touch completely around a joint, a pipe, or any surface area that you want to test. Only touch one area at a time. Immediately after touching each surface, closely inspect the dry finger for any trace of water. Always be careful of sharp or pointed surfaces that could cut or puncture you.

When I try to explain this important technique to most people, they seem to think I am crazy or that I think they are stupid. Often, people don't understand how important this type of detail is until I demonstrate on the job. Frequently, water runs down the back side of a pipe or otherwise goes unnoticed until careful testing with a dry figure reveals its presence. Sometimes people carelessly contaminate a test area by trying to test too much too fast. The dry finger test provides a way to carefully test one joint, one pipe, or one surface at a time. When I mention testing with a dry finger, I am referring to the dry finger test.

Leak investigation is similar to other types of investigation.

- Gather as many facts as possible.

- Try to determine what took place when the leak started.

- Determine if the leak seems to be getting worse or better. Often when I talk to people on the telephone, I ask them to count seconds between drips and try to establish if the drips are getting faster, slower, or, staying the same.

If there is a steady drip (staying the same) sometimes turning the water off the whole house and opening a faucet on the lowest floor (to drain the water) is a good idea. If having the water off seems to clearly affect the leak, there is a good possibility that a water pipe or water pipe connection is leaking.

It is important to check exposed areas very carefully before anyone starts cutting holes in the wall or ceiling. Often it is almost impossible to see leaks that run down the back of a toilet, the back of a supply line, or other surface. If you carefully work a dry finger completely around the back of a toilet, the back of all supply lines, and other surfaces, sometimes, you will find a leak. Do not attempt to feel a leak; each time a dry finger is used to test a surface, the dry finger must be carefully examined for any trace of water. Properly checking for a leak at upper levels is important. Learning to properly test with a dry finger might seem silly, but it is one of the most important things to learn.

Testing a Bathroom Sink for Leaks to the Floor

WITH A DRY finger, check to see if any supply lines, shut-off valve, or any other surfaces have any trace of water; carefully examine your finger after each surface is touched. It is especially important to make sure the back side of supply lines and other surfaces are tested. Always remember to carefully establish the highest surface that fails the dry finger test.

Testing drain connections should be performed thoroughly and systematically:

1. Run hot water in the sink until the drainpipe feels hot.

2. Run cold water in the sink until the drainpipe feels cold.

3. Dry finger test the upper portion of the drain connection (where the drain touches the sink) and proceed to dry finger test all drain connections (always test the highest areas first).

4. Fill the sink with cold water and let it drain out, repeat the testing procedure described in step three.

These four steps provide hot and cold (expansion and contraction) conditions that usually help provide a maximum extreme-testing situation. Filling the sink also helps to provide a maximum extreme-testing situation. If any leaks are found, the procedure must be repeated. Always continue testing until you are sure there are no additional leaks. Sometimes you will find more that one leak.

Testing a Toilet for Leaks to the Floor

1. Dry finger test the bottom of the tank.

2. Dry finger test around the high areas of the bowl and high area around the supply line.

3. Dry finger test the low area of the supply line and the shut-off valve.

4. Dry finger test around the bowl where it touches the floor.

5. Flush the toilet and repeat steps one through four.

6. If there is enough space to slide newspaper under the toilet (without disturbing the toilet), do so and after the toilet is flushed see if the paper gets wet.

These six steps do not properly test the seal under the toilet (AKA the wax seal).

Sometimes, if the drain connection is not visible from below, the only way to check the wax seal is to take out the toilet or cut a hole in the ceiling.

Testing a Bathtub for Leaks Below

IT IS IMPORTANT to start with a dry area. If leaky tile grout, a plumbing leak above, or some other leak runs down to plumbing connections, people automatically assume the connection leaks. As always, it takes systematic testing to focus on one leak at a time.

Testing a bathtub requires a good flashlight and access to the connections at the head of the tub (waste and overflow). Like other testing, it is important to establish a dry area and a dry finger. While the testing procedure will require testing the lowest area first, you must make sure no leaks above contaminate the test area. For example, if there is a grout, caulking, plumbing leak or some other problem above, water might run down; fix it or keep it dry as you systematically test all connections. Even if everything looks perfectly dry, touch all areas with a dry finger to make sure; be careful of sharp edges.

1. Run hot water until the drain feels hot and dry finger test.

2. Run cold water until the drain feels cold and dry finger test.

3. Fill the tub about one-quarter full and drain it. Dry finger test.

4. Fill the tub up to the overflow and make a wave over the overflow. Dry finger test, paying extra attention to the overflow gasket (high up on the tub).

5. Drain the tub and watch for leaks as it drains. After the tub drains dry finger test all connections.

After testing drain connections I usually cap off the shower arm and pressure test the faucet, the pipe between the faucet and the shower arm, and the shower arm.

Often when testing bathtubs, I find more than one leak. All testing procedures need to be repeated until it can be determined that all plumbing connections provide satisfactory results. Frequently, leaky grout, caulking, cracks around the faucet trim, leaky shower doors, or careless people cause leaks.

One of the most important things you can do to save money, aggravation, and time, is to learn how to properly search for leaks. Before you buy a home you should test for leaks.

Before you call a plumber you could search for leaks. After a plumber leaves you might want to test for leaks (depending on the level of trust you have in the plumber).

After a plumber leaves you should make sure that you dry up any water that he might have accidently leaked or splashed while he was working, and then use the dry finger test to determine if you need to call the plumber back to correct a problem. The sooner you let him know, the better. If you find a leak, carefully make sure it is a leak and not just water left over from before the leak was fixed. Ensure that the area is dry and carefully test it at least two times to make sure it is definitely a leak.

Testing after a plumber leaves is extremely important if you used the services of a plumber that doesn't have an established reputation. If you test for obvious problems right after he leaves, that will not guarantee satisfactory long-term results, but testing is much better than nothing.

Toilet Problems

Improperly Flushing Toilet (AKA Poorly Flushing Toilet)

M OST PEOPLE SEEM to know that an obstruction can cause a poor flush. Most people and many plumbers don't realize that there are many factors that control the flush.

- **Obstruction and/or buildup**

- **Proper water level in the tank**

- **Proper water level in the toilet bowl**

- **How quickly water flows from the tank to the bowl**

- **Poorly designed and/or made toilet**

- **Improperly installed toilet**

- **Improper pipe work**

- **Overloading toilets**

An obstruction and/or buildup in the toilet bowl can cause a complete or partial blockage. A partial blockage is a poor flush. Usually this will soon be a complete blockage. An obstruction is usually from an object, an overload, or from gradual buildup. Sometimes the wax seal between the bowl and the floor flange can cause an obstruction. Too much wax and/or misalignment can choke the flow.

The proper water level in the tank is controlled by the ballcock (AKA fill valve) being in proper working order and properly adjusted. Most toilets require that the water level in the tank be five-eighths of an inch to one inch lower than the top of the overflow pipe.

The proper water level in the toilet bowl can be determined by slowly pouring water into the bowl. Pour slowly and gently as pouring too quickly can cause the toilet to flush. When the water in the bowl gets high enough to begin draining down and out, it has reached the *proper water level* (the maximum before it begins to drain). After determining the proper water level, steps can be taken to insure the proper water level is maintained after each flush. The most common factors that cause problems with the water level in the toilet bowl are:

- **Amount of time the flush valve stays open.** Most flush valves stay open long enough after the flush to help refill the bowl. The amount of time the flush valve stays open is different on various flush valves. Some toilets require that the flush valve stays open longer than others (some are adjustable). New toilets always come with the correct flush valve. Sometimes I find that someone has replaced the flush valve with an incorrect one. Sometimes I find that someone has replaced a part on a flush valve with an incorrect part (i.e., flapper). People don't seem to realize that some parts work on the majority of flush valves, but some flush valves require special flappers or other parts. Proper flush-valve timing requires proper parts.

- The **amount of water the refill tube squirts down the overflow pipe** helps refill the toilet bowl. If insufficient water is flowing from the refill tube, make sure it isn't kinked. If that is not the problem, you will have to adjust, repair, or replace the ballcock.

- **The water level in the toilet bowl before it is flushed** is important. The proper water level must be maintained. For example, often people dump mop water into the toilet and lower the water level, or the water evaporates because the toilet is not used for a long period of time.

How quickly water flows from the tank to the bowl affects the quality of the flush. The most common cause of water flowing too slowly from the tank to the bowl is build up inside the toilet bowl flush holes (the small holes around the inside perimeter of the toilet bowl; also, most toilets have a large flush hole at the inside bottom). I use dental tools to clean the flush holes. If dental tools aren't available, you can use a nail, small screwdriver, or a wire coat hanger. Be careful that you don't accidently mark the toilet bowl (marks are difficult to clean off). Often toilet bowl cleaning tablets placed inside the tank will cause reoccurring clogging of flush holes (the one I hate the most looks like blue jelly). The blue jelly type is very messy to remove, but if the complete tablet is not removed, you will have a reoccurring problem. I have had a few jobs where someone has dropped something down inside the flush valve (obstructing the flow to the bowl). I have picked out, and I have vacuumed parts out of toilets to correct this problem.

Poorly designed and/or made toilets usually require replacement. Some toilets are just not capable of a providing a good enough flush to suit the customer's needs. Also, toilets are pottery, and some-times they have defects.

Improperly installed toilets might develop all sorts of problems. One of the most common problems is misalignment and/or too much wax. I can usually tell if I pull my snake back, and it is loaded with wax. If the problem is just too much wax, often I can clean it out with a special snake. I like a drop-head closet auger for this. If misalignment takes place with the type of wax seal that has a plastic funnel built in, I have to take up the toilet. Even if there is no mis-alignment problem, people seem to have more frequent stoppages when the funnel type wax seal is used because it seems that the fun-nel chokes the flow. Every good plumber I ever asked recommends cutting the funnel off. This funnel creates unnecessary back pressure and can create leaks and other problems.

It is rare that **improper pipe work** causes a poor flush. Some toilets are sensitive to the pressure and flow of incoming water. Cer-tainly clogged or defective waste pipe can also cause problems.

Overloading toilets with too much toilet paper or anything else can create a problem. There is a dramatic difference between various toilets as to the load limits before they stop up and/or begin accu-mulating build up. Often people need to experience a toilet stop-page before they can determine what they can and cannot get away with. Sometimes I have to tell people to "do half your business, flush the toilet and then finish your business." (Sorry, but I had to say it.)

Properly Installed Toilet Details Are Important

THERE ARE DIFFERENT ways to approach any job. Carefully locate an honest, qualified professional or learn enough about the job to either do it yourself or supervise an unqualified person doing it (if local code and restrictions allow these options). One of the most common major mistakes I find is people failing to understand how important details are. People fail to do proper research and assume that they can save money by letting an unqualified person (i.e., a tile man, a carpenter, or handyman) install a toilet, sink, or other plumbing fixture. Sooner or later this gambling usually results in major, unhealthy problems that are very costly.

I strongly recommend that you find a properly licensed and insured, trustworthy plumber to do all of your plumbing work. Please understand that I only provide enough details to illustrate that learning enough to properly supervise is beyond the capability of most people. Please do not think that I can provide every necessary detail. Please realize that misunderstandings, errors, omissions and other problems can result in unsafe conditions. Too tight- and -too loose- are examples of details I do not even attempt to address as I provide samples of important details. Often- over tightening will cause cracks or other problems-sooner or later. Explaining how tight is too tight and explaining at what point is too loose, is impossible. I cannot provide enough details to make it safe for you to do it yourself. I cannot provide enough details for you to properly supervise an unqualified worker.

One of the most frequent mistakes is a poorly installed toilet. Often a very nice floor is ruined by a poorly installed toilet. More importantly, major structural, ceiling, and wall damage often result from undetected leaks. I hope I can make you understand how important details directly affect long-term results.

I listed some of the most important details involving the replacement of a toilet. You could use this as a check list. Please be prepared to read some details that will conflict with information you read or saw on television. I provide advice (opinion) based on tried and proven techniques. Please research my qualifications as a plumbing expert and then consider what value you place on my opinions of the best course of action to take. Please read all disclaimers and remember that what works for me might not work for others. All local codes and regulations supersede my advice.

If you plan to have your old toilet reset there are important considerations:

1. Sometimes it is not necessary to separate the tank and the bowl when you take up and reset an old toilet. If the tank and the bowl are separated, all rubber seals should be replaced. Usually it is best to replace old working parts if you are reusing an old toilet.

2. Careful inspection of the toilet will only be possible after the toilet is removed. Cracks and other defects might be discovered after it is removed, so you might want to have a new toilet available.

3. Reusing an old toilet requires extra labor (cleaning, inspection, and replacing old parts).

4. Any old parts could fail at any time.

Normally (because of recent improvements), a new, carefully selected toilet is a wise choice.

To Remove a Toilet:

1. Turn off the water supply to the toilet and disconnect the supply line (catching water as necessary in a container).

2. Remove all water in the toilet.

3. Remove the tank (recommended but often optional).

4. Remove the nuts that hold the bowl to the floor; sometimes they must be cut off.

5. Remove the bowl.

6. Make sure that the shut off valve is 100 percent off.

7. Stuff a balled up, tight fitting, plastic bag inside the floor flange if the toilet will only be removed for a very short period of time. If the toilet will be removed for a longer period of time install a code-approved temporary plug.

8. If the toilet will only be removed for a very short period of time, cover the shut off valve to prevent trash from getting inside the outlet. If the toilet will be removed for a longer period of time, install a code-approved water-tight cap.

9. Clean and dry all surfaces.

To properly install a toilet:

Make sure all surfaces are properly cleaned and dried.

Check the flange, toilet, and all connecting parts for damage or defects.

1. Make sure that the flange is resting at the finished floor level. Often people add new floors that make the flange too low. If the flange is more than one inch too low, you should properly extend it (later extra wax can be added to make up for one inch or less).

2. Install solid brass 5/16" bolts secured to the flange with two nuts (only comes with two, so you will have to purchase two extra nuts)

3. Set the toilet bowl down on the 5/16" bolts (for a test).

4. Make sure that the toilet bowl is reasonably level and add temporary shims if necessary.

5. Make sure that the 5/16" bolts are the proper length (check with washers, nuts, and bolt cover retainers).

6. Mark the toilet bowl and shims with a pencil (to help alignment later).

7. Lift the bowl back off of the bolts.

8. Coat all surfaces that will touch the wax ring with wax (make sure that every square inch sticks).

9. If the flange is one inch or less too low, build up the flange to make up for the difference (sometimes one extra wax seal will do it, but if necessary, press the extra wax seal down so you don't make it too high). Too much wax can cause choking problems.

10. If your wax seal has a plastic funnel type insert, cut out the restricting section, leaving some plastic embedded in the wax; this plastic will help hold the wax in place.

11. Cut a drinking straw in half, split the ends, and slide each end over the 5/16" bolts to extend them. This will allow you to aim the toilet and drop it down properly centered without disturbing the wax seal. Disturbing the wax seal will greatly affect its ability to provide a long- lasting seal.

12. After the wax seal is properly placed on the flange (it is optional, if you want to put the wax seal on the bottom of the toilet, but most good plumbers I have known, put it on the flange), carefully drop the toilet down using the drinking straws to help aim and guide you.

13. Remove the drinking straws and check the alignment (with the pencil marks).

14. Place the bolt cover retainers and metal washers on the 5/16" bolts. Screw the nuts on these bolts but don't tighten them yet.

15. Make sure the toilet bowl settles down against the temporary shims (if shimming was necessary). If necessary, carefully push or sit on the bowl to make it settle down reasonably level.

16. Mix plumber's epoxy putty and carefully fill in gaps between the toilet bowl and the floor. I like to use epoxy putty that is white because most toilets are white. I normally use epoxy putty that gets hard in five minutes, so I mix small amounts individually as needed. Epoxy putty must be installed before it begins to harden, only mix as much as you can use in a timely manner. If you work too slowly and the epoxy putty begins to harden, it is better to stop and mix a fresh batch. Soft epoxy putty carefully installed can provide perfect shimming; improperly installed epoxy putty will create problems. For example, too much epoxy putty or epoxy putty that begins to harden can raise the toilet bowl and create problems. As soon as enough epoxy putty gets hard enough to hold the toilet reasonably level, remove the temporary shims and replace the temporary shims with epoxy putty. There are various methods of shimming. I find that epoxy putty provides a perfect fit. The epoxy can be cut out if the toilet ever has to be taken out.

17. Fill enough gaps to securely hold the toilet reasonably level. Latex caulk can be used to dress up and make the base neat; leave some weep holes for possible leak detection.

18. Tighten nuts and install the bolt covers. Do not over tighten. (Not as tight as nuts on an automobile.)

19. Install the toilet tank according to manufacturer's instructions.

20. Carefully install the water supply line.

21. Check all instructions that came with the toilet and make necessary adjustments.

22. Flush repeatedly and carefully test for any leakage or needed adjustments.

My intention in providing these details is to illustrate important details that are often overlooked.

As I use the word *you* to denote the person doing the work. The person doing the work should be qualified to do it properly and legally. These details can be used as a checklist and should help you focus on the most important details (listing every detail is impossible). Details are important when you compare prices. Details are important if you need to oversee the work as it takes place. Details directly affect long-term results.

As always, your best chance of the most desirable results will be if you can find an honest, highly qualified plumber. That type of a plumber probably will not need these details (although he might benefit from them). These details are intended to help increase the likelihood of the best results. They do not guarantee good results and do not substitute for any local licensed plumber's advice, local governing official advice, or any other qualified local authority. My intentions are to inform readers of details that in my opinion provide the best chance for favorable long-term results.

Miscommunication, failure to follow directions correctly, defective material, and other factors can dramatically affect results. I cannot be responsible for bodily injury, unhealthy conditions (i.e., mold, sewer gas, insects, etc.), property damage, or any other damages or loss that anyone might blame on my information and/or details. Please read other disclaimer information.

Be Careful with Your Toilet
Help Avoid Toilet Stoppages:

- Nothing but toilet paper should be placed in a toilet. No dental floss, cigarette butts, Flushables, etc. NOTHING but TOILET PAPER. [A possible exception is flushable wipes. See my section about flushable wipes.]

- Sanitary napkins should never be flushed, and that includes so-called flushable sanitary napkins, which swell and cause major problems.

- Nothing that could fall into or on the toilet should be stored close to or over the toilet.

- Maintain the toilet in proper working order.

- If you have to buy a new toilet, search for the best flushing one (BUT STICK WITH THE GRAVITY TYPE).

- Focus on details when selecting a new toilet and when selecting the plumber that will install it.

Are Flushable Wipes Safe to Flush?

BECAUSE I NOTICED that some of my customers have stoppages caused by flushable wipes, and many people need to flush these wipes for personal sanitation reasons, I did a carefully monitored study.

My study has unique elements that provide testing under real-life conditions. The conditions necessary for the best testing include:

- A properly piped out plumbing system (including the sewer)

- A properly installed 1.6 gallon toilet

- A properly maintained toilet

- Careful monitoring to assure proper use of the toilet and other plumbing in the home (misuse could cause a blockage that might be blamed on the wipes).

- Carefully following instructions printed on the flushable wipes package.

I personally conducted my study in my home. Using a 1.6 gallon toilet that I installed in the home my wife and I built, I carefully monitored my results. Because I piped out this home, closely monitored the installation of the septic system, and properly maintain the toilet, I know the necessary conditions for a fair test were met. Using every different brand of flushable wipes I could find, I continue to test. So far, it has been over three years, and I have not experienced a blockage or any other problem.

Before my study, I use to advise against flushing these wipes. Now, because of my study, I changed my opinion. It seems that it is reasonably safe to flush these wipes if:

1. The package is clearly marked flushable.

2. Flushable wipes are only placed in a toilet bowl that otherwise has nothing but water in it (no fecal matter, toilet paper, or anything else).

3. No more than two wipes per flush.

4. The toilet, pipe work, and sewer are in proper working order.

5. The municipal sewer or septic tank system is in proper working order.

6. Care is taken to monitor the flush and make sure no backups occur down stream (in the lower level of the house).

7. You realize that unknown problems could result in flooding.

It is extremely important that people realize that they might experience a flood at any time. If there are any defects in the toilet and/or the plumbing, flushable wipes will greatly increase the chances of very undesirable results. If people choose to flush these wipes, and if undesirable results occur, I strongly recommend that they take this as a warning and stop.

Dangers from Chemicals and Gadgets:

AUTOMATIC OR ANY other toilet cleaner containing chlorine should not be placed in the toilet tank. Chlorine causes premature wear on rubber and other parts. Keep in mind that this high concentration of chlorine is soaking everything in the tank twenty-four hours a day seven days a week. Tablets and/or jelly type cleaners often clog the small holes in the toilet bowl and frequently cause a very poor flush.

CHAPTER 13

Pull Out Spout Kitchen Faucet Problems

Some of the most frequent problems I notice from the new style pull-out-spout kitchen faucets:

- The vacuum breaker starts leaking unnoticed [Note: these leaks are usually not noticed until after major damage has occurred.]

- The hose or other part starts leaking unnoticed.

- The hose and/or weight tangles or bumps plumbing under the sink and causes a leak that often goes unnoticed.

- A built-in check valve (in the spray handle) clogs or sticks (causes lousy flow).

- A built-in check valve on hot and cold supply inlets clog or stick (causes lousy flow).

- The base of the faucet becomes unstable (sometimes because of poor installation and sometimes because of poor design).

Because the pull-out spout could be left in a sink full of dirty water, back flow protection must be provided (in case the water is turned off at the main).

Explanation: If the pull-out spout was left in a sink of dirty water, and the water main was turned off, dirty water could be sucked into the waterlines and could contaminate the drinking water. A vacuum breaker is a device that breaks the vacuum by allowing air to flow in at a safe location above the sink providing back flow protection. A check valve is a device that only allows water to flow in one direction (also providing back flow protection).

The old style kitchen faucet with a sprayer does not require pulling out the spout to spray. The old style kitchen faucets with a sprayer seem to be far more reliable and safer. The spout acts like a vacuum breaker. The spout provides back flow protection that makes special vacuum breakers and special check valves unnecessary.

It seems that the old style spray type of kitchen faucets have far fewer problems. This style of faucet has a hose that can get caught on things under the sink like the pull-out spout type, but it doesn't have a weight. Not having a weight that can bang plumbing under the sink, removes that risk.

Pull out spout kitchen faucets are getting better. It is important to realize that it takes years of use to prove reliability. As this book goes to publication, I still don't trust this type of faucet (I recommend the old style for my customers that want a sprayer). I think that eventually, manufacturers will solve the problems I worry about and eventually this new style will be as reliable as the old style.

CHAPTER 14

Clogged Heat-Trap Problems on Water Heaters

SOME WATER HEATERS have a heat trap inside the inlet and outlet pipes. The heat trap is a device that helps prevent heated water from escaping the water heater tank unnecessarily. Some heat traps use a plastic ball to trap heated water. Some heat traps use a rubber flap to trap heated water. I have found problems with both of these type heat traps.

If a heat trap gets clogged, it can result in a major problem. When the heat trap inside the outlet pipe clogs, very little, or no hot water flow can result. This problem can cause inconvenient no hot water flow problems and other problems.

Only properly licensed and insured trustworthy plumbers should attempt to provide temporary or permanent solutions. As always, I only provide information to illustrate and to help you ask the right questions.

Sometimes plumbers can temporarily unclog the outlet blockage if they:

1. Switch the breaker off to the water heater. (If it is a gas water heater, turn the knob to pilot.)

2. Attach a hose to the water heater drain valve (the valve screwed in at the bottom of the water heater).

3. Turn the water off to the water heater (the valve on the inlet (AKA cold) side of the water heater).

4. Squirt water through the hose (into a bucket or other safe place) by quickly turning the drain valve on.

5. Turn the drain valve off (after about two minutes).

6. Turn the water heater inlet valve back on.

7. Open a hot water faucet and run at least ten gallons of hot water.

8. Check the drain valve and make sure it turned off completely.

9. Switch the breaker back on to the water heater. (If it is a gas water heater turn the knob back to on.)

If a heat trap on the inlet side clogs, a dangerous situation can develop very quickly. Usually when the inlet clogs, thermal pressure build up will result in dangerously high pressure. A properly installed safety relief valve (AKA temperature and pressure relief valve) will usually discharge water to the floor or where ever it is piped to if the pressure in the tank is dangerously high. If this safety discharges, you should turn the water heater to pilot or turn the electricity off to it and call a plumber as soon as possible. A discharge from the safety valve can be the sign of a clogged inlet heat trap or other problem. It is important to realize that this safety valve is not intended or designed for day-to-day pressure control. In plumbing terms, the temperature and pressure relief valve is a nonworking valve. That means it should discharge only in an emergency situation. Many plumbers are not aware of inlet heat traps and how they can cause thermal expansion problems. Faulty diagnosis can result from failure to understand how a clogged heat trap can cause dangerously high pressure. Home owners should keep paperwork concerning their water heater readily available for plumbers. Most built in (plastic ball or rubber flap type) heat traps are not visible by looking at the water heater (they are inside normal looking pipes).

The dangers created by these two, most common, heat traps seem to me to illustrate another example of manufacturers failing to consult the right plumbers. Heat traps can be designed to provide energy-saving design while greatly reducing the risk of blockage. I am all for saving energy, but only when products are reliable.

CHAPTER 15

Not Enough Hot Water

"Why doesn't my water heater make enough hot water during cold weather?"

I F YOU NOTICE this problem during freezing weather, often it is due to the extremely cold (ice water) coming in. I call it the "double-whammy affect." People use a much higher percentage of hot water at the shower because they are mixing with ice water. Meanwhile, the water heater takes longer to heat the ice water. It really is the triple-whammy affect. When you use hot water, ice water squirts down into the bottom of the water heater and dilutes about 25 percent of the stored hot water. This also contributes to the short-age. The amount of hot water required, and the amount of hot water available is directly affected by the temperature of the water supply coming in to the home.

If you suspect that an electric water heater is not working prop-erly, many plumbers will do what I call "the old plumber's test."

The test must take place only if you are sure no hot water has been used for at least four hours.

The old plumber's test:

1. He will make sure the proper breaker is off by properly testing the wires (sometimes breakers and fuses are marked incorrectly).

2. He will feel the lower area of the tank (inside the lower access door). If it feels hot, you have a full tank of hot water, and the controls and element work properly.

3. If the lower tank feels cold, he will test the lower element and thermostat (some plumbers will automatically replace the lower element).

Now the old plumber's test for testing the *dip tube* (the pipe inside the tank that carries cold water to the bottom to be heated):

1. He will run about ten gallons of hot water from the water heater (running several faucets for about five minutes).

2. If the lower section of the tank (inside the lower door) cools off, the plumber will tell you that the dip tube is doing its job.

3. If the lower section of the tank (inside the lower door) stays hot, the plumber will tell you that you need a new dip tube. (The cold water is not being properly directed to the bottom.)

I have electronic equipment to test more precisely, but if your heater passes the old plumber's test, most plumbers would probably consider it working okay (and it probably is as long as it provides reasonable temperature control).

Explanation (for those that want to try to understand):

Two element water heaters have a thermostat and a heating element for the top section of the tank and a thermostat and element for the bottom section of the tank. This type of setup will normally satisfy the top thermostat (heat the top) before electricity is supplied to heat the lower element. If the top thermostat or the top element is not in working order, the water heater will provide no hot water. In order for the bottom section of the tank to get hot, the upper element and thermostat must be in working order. In order for the lowest section of the tank to get hot, the lower element and lower thermostat must be in working order. If the lower thermostat or the lower element fails, the lowest section of the tank will not get hot (only the top half of the tank will get hot). All electric controls and elements must be in working order before the lowest section of the water heater tank can get hot. This is why the old plumber's test usually provides satisfactory results.

If the water heater is the single element type (only has a lower heating element), the single element and thermostat must be in working order if the tank is hot; otherwise the water heater would provide no hot water.

The old plumber's test for gas water heaters is much different than that for electric water heaters. There are too many complicated but necessary safety concerns testing a gas water heater. I shall not even attempt to explain all of these important testing procedures.

One water heater test that is easy for most adults to do:

1. Make sure no hot water has been used for at least four hours.

2. Check the water heater label to determine the capacity (gallons).

3. Using a bathtub faucet or other fast flowing faucet, use a five-gallon bucket to measure the amount of hot water that comes out before the hot water runs out.

4. Make a note of how much hot water you ran before it dramatically cooled down.

5. Make a note concerning how many gallons you ran before the water got uncomfortably cold.

Don't expect to get the capacity indicated on the water heater label. (Hot water is diluted with cold as the dip tube squirts cold water into the bottom of the tank.) Depending on how cold the water is coming from the water main to the water heater, you will probably only get about 75 percent of the capacity of the water heater in hot water. If you have a fifty-gallon capacity water heater, you will probably only get about thirty-seven and one-half gallons of hot water if everything is working properly. If you test properly and only get about twenty-five gallons, there is probably something wrong. If you determine that your water heater is not operating properly, call a plumber. A trustworthy plumber should perform necessary testing to determine the best course of action to take.

Often I find that people waste lots of hot water

WASTING HOT WATER is expensive and confusing. Efficient use of hot water is the key to providing a reasonable amount of time for showers. I find more cases of people wasting hot water than I find of malfunctioning water heaters.

If you invest a little time testing for wasted hot water you might save lots of money while you enjoy longer showers.

Using a five-gallon bucket, you should go to each showerhead and spray into the bucket for one minute. Keep track of how much water each showerhead sprays per minute (one-half bucket = two and one-half gallons, etc.). If a showerhead is over a bathtub, after testing the showerhead, place the empty bucket under the spout while water is being diverted to the showerhead. Figure how much water is being wasted (if any) by a defective diverter. Doing some simple math should help you understand, what to expect from your water heater. Efficient use of hot water will provide dramatically better results than purchasing a larger water heater.

Factors to consider:

- A wasteful showerhead (adjust or replace)

- A bathtub diverter that wastes water through the spout while you are taking a shower (repair or replace)

- People might have to take showers faster during cold weather

- A trickle down shut-off valve installed on the showerhead, can save lots of hot water (the showerhead only trickles while you are scrubbing)

- Avoid taking a shower within two hours of washing clothes or dishes

"What is your opinion regarding the new instantaneous water heaters?"

I SHALL ONLY FOCUS on the whole-house type, since I think that is what the question concerns. (There are small instantaneous water heaters that are perfect for isolated sinks often found in offices, warehouses, and other situations.)

So far, I have heard more complaints than I have heard praise. I have never sold one, and too many improvements are needed before I would recommend one. I will explain some technical aspects behind my advice.

If the focus is on an almost endless supply of hot water and not necessarily on saving money, one of these heaters might be useful (if you understand the limitations of various models). I think that if one is properly[1] used in a combination with a properly insulated hot water storage tank, it can provide an almost endless (for practical purposes) supply of hot water. Because the storage tank/instantaneous heater combo would probably provide better results than an oversize conventional water heater, the storage tank could be much smaller. (I have designed a proposal for this, but I consider it experimental.) The only complaint I have heard concerning the stand-alone instantaneous water heaters is regarding temperature changes, and theoretically, a properly utilized storage tank could fix that problem.

An explanation of why I think people have problems adjusting to this highly efficient plumbing product

MOST PEOPLE SEEM to notice at least three changes in the water temperature. These heaters adjust very quickly to accommodate different temperatures of water coming in, but many people seem to have trouble adjusting to the way these heaters provide hot water. The first temperature change is the same as what happens with a traditional water heater, water in the pipe between the water heater and the plumbing fixture is usually room temperature up until the time when the hot water begins to arrive. With a traditional water heater, once the hot water arrives, the temperature usually feels relatively consistent. Instantaneous heaters first heat room temperature water (water that is in the pipe between the heater and the ground). The first shot of hot water is hotter than what immediately follows. As the first shot of much cooler (ground temperature is usually forty degrees) water reaches the heater, the heater quickly adjusts to accommodate this water. After a few seconds, the heater will provide a steady consistent flow of water at the established tem-

---

1   Proper use includes, properly piped out, properly protected, in compliance with all local codes and regulations, etc.

perature. (But it seems that the temperature change is noticeable.) People tell me that they don't like this extra temperature changing process. Lots of energy expense can be saved with these heaters. I am not sure if people will save money. If the initial extra expense, the possible decreased reliability, and possible shorter life span are figured in, a high-efficiency traditional water heater might save more money. (As always, these are just my opinions).

CHAPTER 16

Avoid Water Damage and Avoid Insurance Claims

Insurance Claims: Avoiding Water Damage and Avoiding Reoccurring Damage

I N THIS SECTION I explain some basic principles of maintaining a safe plumbing system. You can use this information to greatly improve your chances of avoiding major water damage. (As always, desirable results are not guaranteed.) A lot of money can be saved, and aggravation and inconvenience can be avoided.

When people ask me what they can do to avoid plumbing problems, I answer, "You can start thinking of your plumbing the way you think of your car; pay a fair price for reliability, be careful who you trust to work on it, and properly maintain it."

1. Before people buy a house they should have it checked out by a licensed plumber that specializes in home plumbing problems. Most home inspection services that I have

observed do not even come close to properly checking plumbing.

2. Be careful about what plumbing products are installed in your home. Ask a trustworthy plumber to provide advice concerning the quality of plumbing products in your home.

3. Always do what ever you can to only use the most reliable plumbing products in your home. Place the highest amount of value on the advice of the most trustworthy plumber you can find as you search for quality plumbing products.

4. Always be aware that reliability requires proper installation and maintenance. The most reliable plumbing fixtures become dangerously unreliable when improperly installed or improperly maintained.

One of the first things people can do to avoid major water damage is to make a list of the places in the home where failure is most likely to occur.

1. Any plumbing that is exposed to freezing weather must be properly winterized and/or protected.

2. All plumbing work that was performed by anyone other than a trustworthy plumber should be considered risky at best (long term and short term). Carefully monitor and/or have questionable plumbing work redone by a trustworthy plumber.

3. Any plumbing fixtures or connections that a trustworthy plumber considers dangerously unreliable should be carefully monitored and/or replaced.

4. Try to identify any frequently occurring plumbing problems neighbors might have experienced. Sometimes defective

water pipes, sewers, or other plumbing problems are common to a neighborhood (same builder, same code defect, or other common elements).

As you begin to see how important a trustworthy plumber is, you should also understand why it is important to avoid emergency situations that often result in questionable repairs by whoever you can get at the time. Most trustworthy plumbers stay very busy and are often not available for emergencies. Emergencies usually occur after business hours and in desperation most people have to use the services of whoever they can get. Low-quality emergency service can result in reoccurring emergencies.

CHAPTER 17

Virginians Need to Know

What I think is a big secret in Virginia and what I think about it

I N 2004, IN Virginia, the standard of requirements for a person performing plumbing was dramatically lowered. Before that date, a master plumber could send a journeymen plumber or a master plumber out to do plumbing. Customers could expect that the person they were paying to do plumbing had a minimum of four years of experience and had passed a special plumbing test. Customers were paying plumbing labor rates for a person that earned the title plumber, which normally refers to a person that has passed a journeymen or master plumber test.

Now in Virginia, as long as a master plumber will be responsible for the work, and as long as he can supervise over the telephone, the master plumber no longer is required to send a licensed plumber out to do the work. Judging from what people tell me, there are now many "installers," "plumbing installers," "technicians," "plumbing technicians," and other people doing a large percent of the plumbing work in Virginia. I think it's important to be aware that these workers have not fulfilled the requirements to become what I call "a real plumber"; based on my personal experience, very few people are aware of this change.

I am not saying that every properly licensed plumber is a trustworthy plumber. I am not saying that every unlicensed plumber (untested or failed the test) is not trustworthy. I am saying that I think it is important that people are made aware of this major change that took place in 2004. People can decide how much value they place on a plumbing license.

It seems to me that customers need to be made aware of the qualifications of workers. When people compare labor rates and shop for estimates, they need to know the qualifications of the person that will actually do the work. It is important to compare qualifications as you compare prices. When consumers pay plumber labor rates, they should make sure they understand the qualifications of the person they are paying for.

Meanwhile, I think the quality of plumbing in Virginia will suffer. Long term, the plumbing trade will suffer, and eventually people will realize that the change in 2004 was a mistake. I think this mistake took place because governing officials like most people are influenced by trendy, oversimplified, misleading media.

I think the secret in Virginia is another example of how people fail to understand how dangerous it is to think plumbing is so simple that anybody can do it. Sadly, over the years I have witnessed a dramatic change in how people think of a plumber.

The noble image of a tradesman working to protect the health of the nation has been transformed to the image of someone that is supposed to be available twenty-four/seven. People judge plumbers by their willingness to be available when needed. People judge plumbers by their willingness to provide a competitive bid even when they are compared to "plumbers" that aren't even real plumbers. To judge plumbers like this is a big mistake.

The plumbing trade should be respected like it once was. People must realize that all plumbers are not the same, but workers that earn the title should at least be recognized for their dedication.

Think of young people considering the plumbing trade and think about how these issues affect them. How misplaced values and unfair bargain shopping will produce a short supply of quality plumbers. If quality plumbing didn't protect the health of the nation, these concerns would not matter. If quality plumbing didn't require top-quality plumbers, it wouldn't matter. In the long term, all of these factors will make a difference.

Cost-Effective Improvements That Should Help You Avoid Problems

Improvements that will reduce Plumbing problems

AFTER PEOPLE LEARN how important taking control of plumbing problems is, they begin to understand that there are cost-effective improvements from which they can benefit. Of course, a local trustworthy plumber should always be consulted before any final decisions are made.

People often ask trustworthy automobile mechanics about things that might improve the performance and durability of their car. Some people start using synthetic oil, synthetic grease, or a top-quality air filter if recommended. Major long-term benefits can be realized if people make cost-effective improvements to the plumbing in their home. If your local trustworthy plumber thinks that you are capable, you might be able to make some of these improvements yourself.

I have provided a list of some cost-effective improvements.

1. Shock absorbers on clothes washer hot and cold supply lines are one of the most necessary, cost-effective, and overlooked plumbing products that I see missing in homes. Shock absorbers that attach with hose washer connections are available. They usually attach very easily (if you have space) between the shut-off valve and the supply hose. Shock absorbers provide air space (air is trapped by using rubber and/or a piston). The trapped air provides a shock-absorbing cushion. Electric (solenoid) valves found on clothes washers open and close so fast that they cause a shock. This shock can cause premature failure on the solenoid, the hoses, and on other plumbing. Most people don't realize that this shock (usually called *water hammer* when people hear it) puts tremendous stress on the plumbing system. Even plumbing that is not in the immediate area can be affected. With the use of a pressure gauge, I have seen potentially damaging shock more than twenty feet away from an unprotected clothes washer or dishwasher.

2. There should be a shock absorber on the supply line to every dishwasher. It is not as easy as installing one on a clothes washer, so it is a good idea to add this when the dishwasher is installed. Sometimes it is easy to install later, sometimes not.

3. Make sure you have a thermal expansion tank if you have a pressure reducer[2] or any back flow restriction on your water main. Many jurisdictions have wisely adopted plumbing codes that require a thermal expansion tank if there is a

---

2   When the water pressure in the street is too high, a pressure reducer should be found close to the main shut-off valve in the home. If you see a strange looking device just above your main water shut-off valve, it is probably a pressure reducer. Usually this reducer will lower the pressure to seventy pounds or less if it is working properly.

pressure reducer on the water main. Older homes often do not have this important protection. The thermal expansion tank is usually installed close to the water heater. [If you are interested in complicated details concerning thermal expansion, please read on, otherwise, please go to item 4.] When the water heater heats cold water, the cold water expands (requires more space). This is referred to as *thermal expansion*. If this expanding water has no place to go, the water pressure increases until it is released or begins to cool. People that use water as the water heater is heating, provide a place for the expanding water to go. Leaky faucets or other leaky valves, provide a place for expanding water to go. Most pressure reducers have a bypass valve built in. The bypass valve will only provide the expanding water a place to go after the pressure in the home reaches pressure higher than the street pressure. It is important to understand that this results in frequent dramatic fluctuations (AKA spikes) in the water pressure. Many doctors call high blood pressure the silent killer; I call high water pressure the silent time bomb. Few people seem to understand that frequent spikes in water pressure can be even more damaging than constant high water pressure. Premature failure and many other problems throughout the plumbing system result from unnoticed high water pressure or spikes in water pressure. Over the years, far too often, I have noticed the extremely dangerous occurrence of the water heater relief valve discharging because of uncontrolled thermal expansion. Often it is difficult to convince people that this is very dangerous. The water heater relief valve is only supposed to discharge in the case of a severe emergency. Repeated discharging can result in rust and other problems that can render this very important safety valve useless. Thermal expansion tanks provide space for water as it expands. With the proper tank, thermal expansion will usually result in less than a ten-pound increase in pressure.

In situations where a thermal expansion tank is needed but not installed, pressure will often more than double.

4. When your water heater is replaced make sure a pan is placed under the new water heater. If reasonably possible, have the pan piped out to a safe location.

5. If an old toilet (two gallon or more) ever needs to be taken out and reset, replace it with a new toilet recommended by a trustworthy plumber.

6. If a shut-off valve is replaced, install a new one-quarter-turn valve recommended by a trustworthy plumber.

7. If a flood occurs because of a low quality part, tell your trustworthy plumber about any similar parts that might be in your home.

8. If a flood occurs because of low-quality plumbing work, tell your trustworthy plumber about any additional plumbing work that you think the same person did.

9. If you ever notice wobbling and/or rocking of a toilet when you sit on it, consider resetting or replacing the toilet.

Always check with a local trustworthy plumber and with your local government regulators, before making any final decisions concerning plumbing improvements or any other plumbing work.

CHAPTER 19

Pinhole Leaks

Pinhole Leaks in Copper Water Pipe

USUALLY, A PINHOLE leak is a leak that is a small drip, a small squirt that looks like a cobweb, or anything in between.

When a pinhole leak occurs in copper water pipe, most people become very concerned. People, hope to avoid future leaks, want to know why the leak occurred, and want to know the best course of action. When my customers ask for my opinions about these concerns, I try to answer their questions as clearly as is reasonably possible. After I examine a pinhole leak, I can make an educated guess as to why it occurred.

Damage from a nail or screw is usually easy to determine. The nail or screw is usually obvious. If you have to have a pinhole leak, this is probably the best one to have. It should be the easiest to avoid and the least likely to become a reoccurring problem.

A poorly made solder joint is usually easy to determine. I always cut out the whole joint. When solder fails to fill the inside of the joint, or if the pipe isn't properly inserted in the joint, the result is a poorly made solder joint. Improperly cleaning, fitting, fluxing, applying the solder, and/or heating of the joint usually results in this problem. It is possible that a plumber's helper or apprentice caused one or two poorly made solder joints, sometimes complications and future problems will not develop. Poorly made solder joints can be a big problem if lots of joints were poorly made. Some concerns about poorly made solder joints include:

1. Other solder joints were probably made by the same person that made the joint being replaced. Additional poorly made solder joints could start leaking at any time.

2. Solder joints in the immediate area will have to be disturbed to replace the leaky one. Correcting one leak could easily result in more leaks.

3. Poorly made solder joints can blow apart and result in a major flood at any time.

4. Often, poorly made solder joints look fine (what is important is what is inside the fitting).

It seems that most people with a poorly made solder joint leak do not have reoccurring problems. If it looks like a plumber did the soldering, I usually recommend replacing only the joints that leak. If it looks like someone other than a plumber did the soldering, I usually recommend replacing all easily accessible solder joints. Hindsight is always twenty/twenty, so it is important to realize that predicting the outcome is not an exact science, there is no way to know the best course of action every time. (If the plumber is right 99 percent of the time, it is guaranteed that he will be wrong 1 percent of the time.) If an honest, qualified plumber makes an educated guess or presents the available options, so you can decide how much pipe work to replace, you shouldn't blame him if things go terribly wrong.

Sometimes, it is easy to determine that the copper pipe was **electrolyzed** (decomposed by the direct action of an electric current). Most plumbers realize that dissimilar metals that touch can create a damaging electrical current (AKA **electrolysis**), and because of this, it is necessary to protect copper water pipe (or galvanized water pipe) from coming in contact with **dissimilar metal**. This extremely low electric current produced from dissimilar metals **should not be confused with the dangers of electrical current flow from the electric power in the home.** I have concerns about **a different danger from** possible **electric power** in the home.

I have a **theory** that since many homes use the **copper water pipe as a ground**, it is even more important to make sure the copper water pipe does not come in contact with duct work, gas pipe, or other possible metal objects that could interrupt the proper electrical (grounding) flow. I have seen pinholes where copper pipe touches ducts. I worry about copper water pipe touching metal gas pipe.

If dissimilar metal straps or any other dissimilar material is the most likely cause of a leak (this is usually visible when the leak is located) something should be done to correct the problem. Even before problems occur, copper water pipes should be protected from all other metal. Often, thinking ahead and using common sense can prevent dangerous situations from causing problems.

Pinhole leaks in copper pipe that seem to have developed for no reason are becoming a major problem in some areas. Some of the reasons seem to be:

1. Chemicals in municipal water attack the copper. Typically, most of the pipe will look fine. White or green spots will be visible. The pipe will be stable enough to easily cut.

2. Aggressive well water. Aggressive well water often results in paper-thin copper pipe. Fixing one area often requires extensive replacement as pipes are very fragile. [Note: CPVC pipe is usually the best replacement, since CPVC seems to hold up much better under aggressive water conditions.]

3. Aggressive flux that was used when the pipes were soldered might cause pinholes. When using the aggressive type flux, pipes and fittings do not require as much cleaning before soldering. Aggressive flux used to be the standard for copper waste and vent pipes. Most good plumbers never used it for water pipe. Some plumbers used it on water pipe to save time. I am beginning to think there is a good possibility that what I call aggressive flux is a frequent cause for pinholes. Aggressive type flux results in lots of green stains on copper pipe while nonaggressive flux causes very little green. [Tip: Aggressive flux on your skin will cause an irritating burning sensation, nonaggressive flux normally will not.] If aggressive type flux was used and not carefully wiped off, it is easy to tell by the large amount of green stains. If it is carefully wiped off, it is very difficult to tell. When I see the inside of pipes that have mysterious pinhole leaks, I often find a small glob of green material.

4. Copper electroplated straps frequently have very sharp edges. Sometimes I find pinhole leaks where the sharp edge of an electroplated strap touches copper pipe. I suspect that the sharp edge eventually cuts into the pipe, or the edge exposes enough steel (the core of copper electroplated straps is steel) to allow electrolysis to create a hole. [Note: I have never noticed a solid copper strap creating a leak.]

I suspect that there is no simple answer for the increased frequency of mysterious pinhole leaks. I think aggressive flux, applying too much flux, not properly flushing out water pipes, chemicals in the water, ageing of the pipes, and any combinations of these factors play a key roll in this problem.

After a pinhole leak is fixed, it is not possible to know when, where or if additional leaks will occur. Usually, I cut out as much stained pipe in the immediate area as I think is reasonably practical. Sometimes I replace a large amount of pipe, and sometimes, I cut directly over the pinhole and install a coupling (this usually requires the least amount of expense and the least amount of disturbance to the pipes). Whenever reasonably possible, I try to explain options to the customers so they can decide what they want me to do. Lots of time and money can be spent in one area only to notice additional leaks in the next area. Disturbing defects can cause leaks; sometimes the more work performed, the more risk is involved. The only way a customer should expect the plumber to guarantee no more leaks from the water pipe is if he replaces all the pipes.

Research and customer communication can help provide the best chance for the most cost effective solution. The more information the customer can gather, the better.

Some of the factors to research include:

- The number of homes in the same development that have had reoccurring leaks.

- The number of reoccurring leaks in the customer's home.

- What information is available from the local water supplier?

- The number of homes in the same development that had all the water pipes replaced.

- The age of the pipes.

- The projected time before major renovation of the home is expected.

- When does the owner expect to sell the home?

- The financial ability of the customer.

In most cases, customers should only expect the plumber to fix the immediate problem. The more pipes are disturbed, the greater the possibility of creating additional leaks. Plumbers have a very difficult time figuring how many customers they can help in one day. There is no way to know how long each job will take. Customers should realize that sometimes scheduling at least one additional visit might be necessary. Usually the initial visit is intended to help the customer get the water back on or get a leak under control.

Sample details concerning estimating a job that is too small to estimate

An Estimate to Replace a Wax seal on a Toilet

To HELP ILLUSTRATE why many trustworthy plumbers do not try to estimate small plumbing jobs, I have prepared some important details concerning an estimate to take out and reset a toilet (AKA replace a wax seal). This information is not intended to represent a complete contract or to illustrate every possibility. The times listed do not represent how an actual job took place or an exact description of how much time would be required.

This information is intended to focus on enough of the frequently occurring complications and necessary details to provide an example of why estimates, set prices, and, educated guesses for small plumbing jobs are often of little value. Prices can change, and one plumber may carefully focus on details while others cut corners and skip details. Trustworthy plumbers focus on your best interest while others focus on ways to increase their profits.

Trustworthy plumbers try to avoid misleading customers. Trustworthy plumbers don't try to hide important details in fine print. Less than trustworthy plumbers often use fine print to hide important information. When the cost of complications can dramatically change the estimate price, most trustworthy plumbers realize that the estimate is not practical.

This price includes all necessary labor and material to take out and reinstall a toilet **if no complications develop**.

This proposed price (AKA estimate) includes:

1. Get necessary protective covers (for the floor), parts, and tools to the bathroom. (Twenty minutes.)

2. Turn off the water to the toilet (**assuming** the shut-off valve works properly). (One minute or less.)

3. Remove the water from the tank and bowl. (Five minutes.)

4. Remove covers (aka china caps) and unscrew the nuts that attach the toilet to the floor flange (AKA closet flange). (**Assuming** that the nuts unscrew with no difficulty, one minute or less.)

5. Cut any caulking or other material that might make the toilet stick to the floor. (**Assuming** this will be easily removed, five minutes or less.)

6. Lift the toilet up off the floor and set it in a location, so the bottom can be cleaned and dried. (**Assuming** there is enough open floor space to do this in the immediate area, two minutes or less.)

7. Do a brief inspection of the toilet, floor flange, and pipe, searching for any easily visible defects. (**Assuming** the

customer understands that there is no guarantee that all defects will be noticed, allow five minutes or less.)

8. Remove the bolts that attach the toilet to the floor flange. (**Assuming** there are no complications, one minute or less.)

9. Clean the flange and the area that was covered by the toilet. (**Assuming** that this can be done easily, ten minutes or less.)

10. Install new solid brass bolts in the floor flange using two nuts to securely hold these bolts in the proper place. (**Assuming** the flange is properly located in the floor and properly aligned with the wall, two minutes.)

11. Test every square inch of the floor flange to make sure wax will stick readily and then, coat every square inch of the floor flange with wax. (Three minutes or less.)

12. Test every square inch of the bottom of the toilet where the wax seal will touch to make sure wax will stick readily. Coat this same area with a thin layer of wax. (Three minutes or less.)

13. Firmly place the new wax seal on top of the floor flange. (**Assuming** the floor flange is at the proper height in relation to the finished floor, three minutes or less.)

14. Set the toilet down over the new bolts while being extra careful to not disturb the wax ring. Make sure the toilet is settled down to the lowest point where it will be reasonably level and reasonably aligned with the wall. (**Assuming** there are no defects in the floor, ten minutes or less.)

15. Shim (provide hard material in enough spots around the base of the toilet to make up for gaps) the toilet as necessary to prevent future wobble. (**Assuming** it only requires a normal amount of shimming, ten minutes or less.)

16. Attach cap holders, washers, and nuts on bolts attached to the floor flange. (Three minutes or less.)

17. Attach water supply line to toilet. (Three minutes or less)

18. Turn water shut-off valve on and test the shut-off valve, the supply line, and the toilet for leaks. (**Assuming** no leaks are found, six minutes or less.)

19. Test the toilet for proper operation and check for any obvious malfunctions or defects. Make minor adjustments as needed. (**Assuming** the customer understands that there are no guarantees on old parts or toilets, and that only minor adjustments are needed, ten minutes or less.)

20. Recheck for leaks. If a small leak is found at the shut-off valve, an attempt will be made to tighten the packing (the seal on the stem) and about ten minutes later, it will be tested again. (The ten-minute testing period will take place while clean up and organizing takes place, so the ten minutes is not added to this testing time.) (Four minutes is allowed for the recheck mentioned above.)

Later, if it is necessary to repair or replace the shut-off valve, it will cost extra money (**just like any other complication will cost extra money**). Most likely, the water supply to the whole house will have to be turned off and drained to make it possible to repair or replace the toilet shut-off valve. The cost of this extra work is unknown. Problems with the main shut-off valve and/or other complications may or may not develop. (The main shut-off valve might work perfectly and later pass the leak test or it might have the same problem as the toilet shut-off valve had.)

This proposal assumes the customer wants to take out an old toilet and reinstall the toilet. It is also assumed that the customer is attempting to keep the cost to a minimum by attempting to have a minimal amount of work provided.

It is important to realize, that **sometimes an attempt at keeping expense as low as possible can result in just the opposite.**

For example, often an old toilet can be taken out and reinstalled without separating the tank from the bowl. Money for new rubber seals and the cost of the required extra labor might be saved. Frequently, money is saved by doing the work this way. Some times after the old toilet is reset, seals between the tank and bowl start leaking. When this happens the customer will have to pay more than if the tank had been removed as part of the original estimate price.

Some people like to rush to decisions and then blame the plumber. When complications occur, people say they think they should have been warned about the possible complications. It is often impossible to provide every possible combination of complications. What makes it even more difficult is that the majority of the time, no complications will develop.

Many customers say the plumber "talked the job to death" or "couldn't give me a straight answer" or they find it hard to trust a plumber that won't provide an estimate. Some customers get aggravated when they don't get simple answers, simple prices, and simple guarantees. These customers often bad mouth trustworthy plumbers or do what some call shoot the messenger when they don't like the message.

Depending on the age, condition, quality, appearance, and other factors, often it is a good idea to install a new toilet if you have to remove and reset an old toilet (as long as you select the new toilet carefully). Trustworthy, expert advice should help you select a new toilet that uses less water, provides a better flush, and is more reliable than most old toilets.

For people that are determined to keep their old toilet and determined to shop for estimates, I made a list of **optional specifications.** Take out and reset the toilet:

- Option 1: Do not separate the tank from the bowl or replace any of the working parts (If any parts leak or fail to work properly during the final testing, they will be replaced at an extra expense. It is understood that any old part could fail or leak at any time.)

- Option 2: Separate the tank from the bowl and replace seals and bolts that hold the tank to the bowl and the seal between the tank and the bowl. (If any parts leak or fail to work properly during the final testing, they will be replaced at an extra expense. It is understood that any old part can fail or leak at any time.)

- Option 3: Do not separate the tank from the bowl; replace the fill valve (AKA ballcock) and flapper. (If any parts leak or fail to work properly during final testing, they will be replaced at an extra expense. It is understood that any old part can fail or leak at any time.)

- Option 4: Separate the tank from the bowl and replace seals and bolts that hold the tank to the bowl, the flush valve, the fill valve (AKA ballcock) and the seal between the tank and the bowl. (If any parts leak or fail to work properly during the final testing, they will be replaced at an extra expense. It is understood that any old part could fail or leak at any time.)

If customers can understand all of the **assuming** illustrates the possibility of added expense, I think it is easy to see that estimating small jobs like this is not practical. Even with all these possible complications, sometimes this work will be completed with none. On average, I would say all these details (if no complications) could be properly attended to in about two hours. Normally, there will be at least one small complication that requires extra time, so two and one-half hours might be a more realistic guess at the time needed to do the work properly.

If one major complication or if many small complications developed, there would be a dramatic increase in the required amount of time and the price.

By now, you can probably understand why many trustworthy plumbers don't try to estimate small jobs. By charging customers for the actual time spent solving their plumbing problems, unnecessary wasted time and confusion are avoided.

My example concerning replacement of a wax seal uses a small job that most people can understand. Some small jobs are much more difficult to place a value on.

It is difficult for people to know the difference between a reasonable price and an outrageous price for replacing a leaky pipe. The risk of complications and the amount of focusing on important details becomes more complicated when trusting a plumber to provide a price to replace a section of leaky pipe. Often, I hear of outrageous prices people were charged to have a leaky pipe replaced. People request a price, they agree to the price, and the work is done. Later, they complain that the work was completed in a very short amount of time, and they were charged an outrageous amount of money. When people ask me how they should deal with plumbers that charged outrageous prices, I usually tell them to learn from their mistakes. The only way to know if you get your money's worth is to know you are dealing with a trustworthy plumber and keep track of the time he spends solving your problem.

Some trustworthy plumbers only work for people that agree to pay for his actual time at the home and for the parts, fixtures, and other material he supplies. The term for this type of an arrangement is time and material (AKA T&M). As long as customers deal with trustworthy plumbers, this is the most cost-effective way to do business. The customer gets what is paid for—no more, no less.

Basically, people are renting the plumber, renting the plumber's truck, and renting his equipment, when they are using his services. (Exception: Most plumbers charge extra if he has to use an electric snake.)

CHAPTER 21

Owner's Manual for the Home

Sample Owner's Manual for Home Plumbing

THIS SAMPLE MANUAL should help you gather and organize the best available plumbing advice, keep track of plumbing work performed in your home, and keep track of plumbing products in your home. This manual will provide a basic format that you and others can use to monitor and maintain the plumbing in your home. A properly constructed manual will provide important, top-quality information before you need it. After you see the benefits of organized top-quality advice, you will make better decisions and avoid most plumbing emergencies.

I call this a sample manual because it isn't the final word. This manual is provided as a starting point. Like everything else you find in this book, it is my opinion. My opinions are based on what I learned and experienced doing plumbing for more than thirty-eight years, but my advice/opinions should not be considered the final word. Information you gather from local governing codes and governing officials supersede what I say. Information you gather from a local trustworthy properly licensed and insured plumber supersede what I say. Before any action is taken, you should verify my advice/opinions locally. Each individual plumbing situation is different, local weather, and other geological conditions are different; it is important to realize that there isn't one simple answer that applies to all homes. Interpretation, miscommunication, failure to follow directions properly, errors and omissions, and other problems can result in hazardous situations. Please read all disclaimers and please realize that I always have the best intentions, but results will not always be desirable.

Start an Owner's Manual for Home Plumbing

1. Buy a binder that has rings to hold pages and pockets to hold receipts.

2. Label the front cover Owner's Manual for Home Plumbing.

3. Use this binder to keep track of who to call, what to do, and when.

4. Keep receipts concerning plumbing products, plumbing work, permits, and any other related products or services in the pockets, or make holes to attach with the binder rings.

5. Use the binder to store warrantees, instructions, and any other papers concerning plumbing in the home.

6. Store this book and any other important plumbing information together alongside the manual.

List the:

- Most desirable trustworthy plumber's name and phone number.

- Well pump specialist (if you have a well)

- Septic tank cleaner (if you have a septic tank)

- Sump pump or any other specialist

- Emergency carpet clean-up or other emergency clean-up specialist

- Most desirable trustworthy emergency (after hours) plumber's name and phone number.

- Gas Company's emergency phone number.

- Water authority's emergency phone number.

- Fire department's nonemergency phone number.

- Fire department's emergency phone number.

These phone numbers should be kept up to date.

By properly maintaining plumbing, the first number listed is probably the only one you will ever call.

Properly maintained plumbing requires the proper development, storage, and use of this manual. This manual can play an important part in helping you do the right thing at the right time. Avoiding plumbing problems and solving small plumbing problems (before they become big ones), can save lots of time, money, and aggravation. More importantly, properly maintained plumbing provides sanitary living conditions.

Think of this manual like you think of the owner's manual for an automobile:

- Keep this manual in an area of your home where it can be easily consulted as needed.

- If you rent your home there should be two copies of this manual (one for the owner and one for the renter).

- If you rent your home using the services of a property manager or other professional, there should be three copies of this manual (one for each of the three parties involved).

- Use this manual to monitor your plumbing in a timely manner.

- Use this manual to gain proper control of plumbing problems, so you can wait for the best plumber and not desperately wait for any plumber that you can get in an emergency situation.

- Use this manual to keep track of plumbing services provided.

Table of contents:

12. Monitoring and testing other plumbing fixtures.

13. How to search for a leak.

14. What to do if...

15. What not to do if...

1. During normal business hours call our normal plumber to schedule services.

   Normal business hours are _____ (Monday-Friday)
   (No Major Holidays)

   Our regular plumber's name is _____

   Phone number is _____

   Always try to control problems and attempt to avoid emergency
situations.

   If time allows, consult this manual to see if it can provide help
locating a shut-off valve or finding another temporary solution.

   If emergency plumbing services are needed during normal business hours, and time allows, request the help of the regular plumber.
If an emergency doesn't allow enough time to wait for a response
from the regular plumber, call the emergency plumber.

   The emergency plumber's name is _____

   Phone number is _____

   The emergency plumber promises to respond in a timely manner:

   Promised response time for a return call is _____

   Promised response time for arrival is _____

   The emergency plumber provides service twenty-four/seven and
all holidays.

2. Try to identify the source of the problem. If you can control the problem by not using a fixture, turning off a fixture, catching the leak before it causes harm, or by some other action, focus on scheduling the services of our regular plumber. If property damage, possible bodily injury, or unhealthy conditions are created by the problem, focus on getting the situation under control in a timely manner. Out of control problems are emergencies. Flooding creates the risk of structure failure, electric shock, and other dangers. Depending on the severity of the flood, various courses of action are recommended. Request the help of an emergency plumber, try to get advice from the regular plumber (if the emergency takes place during normal business hours), or call the fire department. Some localities recommend calling the nonemergency fire department phone number if time allows. (Note: It is a good idea to call the nonemergency fire department number as part of your emergency plan. Your local fire department could explain the types of flooding they consider dangerous.) The nonemergency fire department phone number is _____ The emergency fire department phone number is _____

3. If your home has shut-off valves located on every hot and cold pipe under every sink, you should indicate that here: yes____ no_____, normally, every toilet has a shut-off valve located directly under the tank, if not, indicate that here. If you have shut-off valves to a humidifier, icemaker, dishwasher, or any other device, provide a map to indicate where the valves are located. Place a numbered tag on each of these valves and provide matching numbers on your map. Print a brief description on each tag concerning what it controls.

4. Arrange to have your normal plumber explain details concerning how to properly winterize outdoor faucets. Take notes and provide carefully constructed instructions here. (Note: Details are very important.)

5. Some homes have unique characteristics that require extra attention. Your knowledge of past frozen pipes and how to avoid them could help prevent future problems. Leaving cabinet doors open, not leaving the garage door open, or other necessary information should go here. Many people mistakenly think pipe insulation provides a safe solution against frozen pipes. Pipe insulation can help, but what is more important is keeping cold air away from the pipes. Often, plenty of insulation on the cold side of the pipes, while little or no insulation on the warm side is a better approach. I strongly recommend moving water pipes out of areas that could expose them to freezing temperatures. Moving pipes to a safe area is the best solution. Pipe insulation can delay freezing, but it is not a remedy.

6. When pipes freeze, they often burst. During freezing weather, it is important to make sure that people realize that no flow usually indicates frozen pipe. If pipe stays frozen too long, it will burst and flood after it thaws. It is important to closely monitor frozen pipe and be ready to turn the water off quickly. Finding a plumber with a pipe-thawing machine usually provides your best chance of quickly thawing frozen pipe.

7. Food coloring placed carefully in toilet tanks can help locate toilets in need of repair. If colored water in the tank shows up in the bowl (before flushing), the toilet is wasting water and needs repair. Sometimes careful inspection with a flashlight and a dry finger, will help identify external toilet leaks that could

cause property damage. If water is noticed on the floor, try to determine if it is running down from a higher surface. If a toilet moves when you sit on it, there is a problem. Toilets that move (AKA rock) eventually leak. Toilets must be kept stable so the wax seal and other connections do not get disturbed.

8. Draw pictures and provide instructions indicating the locations of all bathtub access doors. Periodical, careful inspection with a flashlight, and a dry finger can help identify leaks.

9. Make sure all grout, caulking and other cracks are kept filled. Try to make sure shower curtains and shower doors do not allow water to escape the bathtub or shower.

10. Periodically, carefully inspect the area under hand basins with a flashlight and dry finger. If you notice water, try to identify the highest surface that is wet. Be aware that excessive water splashed around the faucet and/or the pop-up assembly push-pull rod, can cause some unavoidable (AKA not fixable) leakage. If excessive splashing causes leaks, tell people to be more careful.

11. Periodically, carefully inspect the area under the kitchen sink with a flashlight and dry finger. If you notice water, try to identify the highest surface that is wet. Try to avoid disturbing pipes when storing items under the sink. Make sure pull-out spray hoses do not disturb pipes, valves, and connections under the sink. Be aware that excessive water splashed around a faucet, sprayer, or other penetrating device, can cause some unavoidable (AKA not fixable) leakage. If excessive splashing causes leaks, tell people to be more careful.

12. Periodically, carefully inspect all plumbing using a flashlight and dry finger. If you notice water, try to identify the highest surface that is wet. If you ever turn a valve (on or off), carefully check for

leakage at the handle (AKA packing nut). (Tip: Often tightening the packing nut will fix this leak, but make sure the leak stops.) Check water heaters, pressure reducers, relief valves, and any other device that could leak.

13.   One of the best ways to test a hand basin, bathtub, kitchen sink, laundry sink, bar sink, or other sink requires a systematic approach. First, run hot water until the drainpipe gets warm (this will cause expansion). Carefully check for leaks using a dry finger. Now, run cold water until the pipe gets cool (this will cause contraction). Carefully check for leaks using a dry finger. Finally, fill with cold water and drain. Carefully check for leaks using a dry finger. If you are testing a bathtub, now you must fill the tub, make a wave over the over flow (or figure out some other way to submerge the overflow), and carefully check for a leaky overflow gasket. Testing bathtub faucets and shower arms for leaks inside the wall is more complicated. Most plumbers cap off or valve off the showerhead and turn the faucet on (with the diverter in the shower position) to test bathtub faucets and shower arms. Most home owners might examine inside the access door, while the shower is running, to see if the faucet leaks inside the wall. The problem with allowing the shower to spray is that leaky cracks in the tile grout and/or caulking might result in confusing test results. Testing for leaks from a shower stall is time consuming and tricky. (Most showers do not have an access door.) If a home owner can carefully stop up the drain pipe from a shower (not the top of the drain but the two-inch pipe inside), some important testing can take place. After the two-inch pipe is stopped up, it is important to carefully pour enough water in the shower pan to cover the shower floor. Do not get the water from the shower being tested; it is important

to fill the container used to transport the test water, from a different source. **This testing must be performed systematically and carefully to assure proper testing and proper evaluation of the results.** It is important that only one area of the shower be tested at a time. The shower faucet should not be turned on until after the shower pan and drain has been tested (test one thing at a time). If water is allowed to stand over the shower floor for twenty minutes or more and there are no signs of leakage below or outside the shower area, most likely, the shower pan and the drain connection do not leak. If leaking is noticed, most likely, the pan and/or the drain connection leak. This test works for one-piece fiberglass, terrazzo, plastic, or other shower pans. This test also works for tile floored shower stalls that normally have a lead pan, PVC pan, or other pan under the tile. If the pan and drain connections pass the first-stage test, it is important to test the trap and other drain connections (the second stage of test). The second stage test requires removal of the stopper that you used to partially fill the pan. Carefully dumping several buckets of water down the drain will help determine if the trap or other pipe connections leak. The third stage of a systematic shower test involves the faucet, riser (AKA pipe to the shower arm), and the shower arm (the pipe the showerhead is screwed to). Most trustworthy plumbers will remove the showerhead and attach a cap, a pressure gauge, or a valve to the shower arm. By turning on the faucet and waiting for about ten minutes, this provides a good test of the shower faucet, riser, and shower arm. Home owners might try to perform this test with out the benefit of closing off the shower arm. Unfortunately, if the shower sprays on a crack, and leakage takes place through the tile or some other crack, the home owner might not know if the faucet, riser, or the shower arm leaks or the crack is causing the problem. Systematic testing is important-but- time consuming, and sometimes results in unnecessary expense. Failure to properly close a shower curtain or maintain tile can result in expensive plumbing bills. Often plumbers are forced to test plumbing to prove that plumbing does not leak. Money can be saved if you can properly and carefully search for leaks.

14. If you notice a leak try to determine what took place that seems to have caused the leak (Example: flushing a toilet, taking a shower, taking a bath, etc.). Try to determine if the leak is getting worse, slower, or seems to have stopped. Sometimes counting the seconds between drips or keeping track of the size of a puddle can help you determine if the leak is getting worse. Try to turn off valves, catch leaks, or find other ways to prevent dangers and property damage. Develop a plan before the plan is needed. Knowing who to call, how to handle emergencies, and understanding how this book can help you locate valves, and do the right thing should greatly improve your chances of the best results.

15. If you notice a leak or a major flood do not panic. Often people make bad decisions and make bad situations worse when they let emotions control their actions. Don't forget that safety is always most important. Be aware of electrical dangers, risk of slippery floors, sharp edges and other risk of bodily harm. **Always focus on safety.**

I hope these basic guidelines inspire you to start an owner's manual for your home. On my Web site, and in future books, I plan to provide more tips and details.

CHAPTER 22

Do It Right or Don't Do It

O FTEN, PEOPLE TELL me that they are thinking about replacing a whole bathroom or a kitchen. Sometimes people say that they are thinking about building an addition to their home. When people ask me for advice concerning these projects, I say, "Do it right or don't do it."

When should you replace the whole Bathroom, Kitchen –or build an addition?

Y OU SHOULD NEVER proceed with any project until after you have completed the proper amount of research (AKA Homework). Most people fail to do very important research properly. People focus on the fun and easy part of the research and often overlook the important boring parts of the research.

Basic and Simple Yet Complicated

T HE MOST IMPORTANT part of a major renovation is the general contractor. Not doing the proper amount of research to find a trustworthy general contractor is a major mistake people frequently make.

Another, often even worse, major mistake is home owners playing the part of general contractor without understanding the duties and responsibilities (many people don't even realize that if they don't have one, they are one). There are many less than honest subcontractors that make big profits from home owners that think they can save money by cutting out the general contractor. It amazes me that so many highly educated people fail to research the duties of a general contractor before they decide if they have the time and skills to do the job.

How important is the General Contractor?

THE GENERAL CONTRACTOR is the most important part of a project. He is more important than the quarterback in American football. He controls what gets done and makes sure things are done in the proper order. The general contractor must properly select subcontractors that work together in a timely manner to properly complete a project. The general contractor has to find subcontractors he can trust. Most trustworthy subcontractors try to only work for general contractors that seem to have the necessary skills to properly organize the project.

An experienced trustworthy plumber realizes that a bad tile man, a bad carpenter, or other bad team member can make him look bad (cause problems that dramatically affect the project). Satisfactory long-term results require that all team members do their job properly. One bad team member can make the whole team look bad; a trustworthy general contractor builds and maintains a trustworthy team of subcontractors.

What makes a General Contractor Trustworthy?

HONESTY, KNOWLEDGE, AND experience are the three most important qualifications to be a trustworthy general contractor (and of course- proper licenses, insurance, bonds, and other legal requirements).

Good communication skills, personality, and many other traits help, but are not as important. (I have known some very trustworthy general contractors that were rude and had other personality flaws but were among the best at getting things done properly at a reasonable price.) Most trustworthy subcontractors and many customers focus more on honesty and professionalism and less on communication skills and personality. Some of the worst general contractors survive only because they have excellent communication skills and appear to have a charming personality.

Usually plumbing should be done by a trustworthy plumber, electrical work should be done by a trustworthy electrician, and each category of work handled by a properly licensed specialist. I often see major problems that result from a good tile man doing bad plumbing, a good floor man doing bad plumbing, or a good countertop man doing bad plumbing. You greatly increase your chances of the best long-term results if you make sure the general contractor will use the correct specialist for each category of work. When comparing prices, you should use a checklist with-at least- minimal requirements.

The General Contractor Checklist

The general contractor shall:

- Use licensed plumbers, electricians, and other specialists for their respective categories of work.

- Be responsible for obtaining any necessary permits.

- Make sure all work passes the required inspections, and he shall be required to make any necessary corrections in a timely manner.

- Make sure he and all subcontractors have proper licenses, bonds, liability insurance, workmen compensation insurance, and meet any other necessary requirements.

- Provide a time line of events and a completion date.

- Provide a list of expected inconveniences (i.e., water off, electricity off, kitchen out of order, bathroom out of order, etc.)

- Provide a time line for expected inconveniences.

- Dust control, daily cleanup, working during normal hours, and other seemingly commonsense elements.

- Explain how he shall remedy and/or pay penalty, if he violates any terms of the agreement.

The General Contractor Checklist I provided is just a minimal amount of details you must consider as you compare prices. Amazingly, many people fail to focus on anything other than price and promises. Focusing on price and promises gets lots of people in trouble.

Nightmare is one word that many use to describe the experience that often results from trusting the wrong people. The nightmare can begin as the work progresses or the nightmare might begin a year or more later. Hopefully, if you focus on finding a trustworthy general contractor, use a checklist to keep the bids honest, carefully review details on contracts, and trust only those worthy of trust, you will avoid costly and inconvenient mistakes and nightmares.

Learn the Job Before You Assume That You Can Do It

SOME OF THE most basic parts of being a general contractor are fun and easy. Television and other media specialize in focusing on fun and easy. I see far too many people making very serious and costly mistakes, based on bad research. Don't allow entertainment to distract you from doing real research. I hope my illustrating some of the truly important parts of general contracting will inspire you to do proper research before you make a major mistake. (I see the results of this type of mistake frequently.)

A general contractor must know enough about every trade to be able to:

- Put together and maintain a trustworthy team of subcontractors.

- Organize subcontractor appearances on the job in the proper order.

- Monitor each job as it takes place.

- Understand what constitutes extra charges by the subcontractor.

- Investigate who is to blame if something seems to have gone.

- Understand how change orders affect the overall project.

- Communicate on a technical level with subcontractors.

- Include important details in all contracts (subcontractors and customers).

What Makes a Bathroom, Kitchen, or Addition Trustworthy?

Selecting trustworthy products and making sure the products are properly installed is the only way to make the end result trustworthy. Do the proper amount of research using trustworthy sources of advice. If you don't have the time and skills to be a trustworthy general contractor, be smart enough to find one. If you can't find trustworthy products and trustworthy professionals to install them, don't do it. You are the most important part of a trustworthy team. You must act responsibly and make sure that you use due diligence as you make key decisions.

Be a Trustworthy Part of the Team

Like it or not- you are a key part of the team. It is important that you, or any partners, establish one person to communicate with other team members (the general contractor and others). Husband and wife partners must decide which of them will be the customer. General contractors and others need to have a single source of contract negotiation and decision making. Major confusion and other problems can be avoided by making sure one person is the established trustworthy customer.

Part of being a trustworthy customer involves D.U.E diligence before searching for bids.

Do proper research

Use your imagination

Estimate the amount of money you can afford for the project

Do proper research by focusing on the best available trustworthy advice.

Use your imagination to visualize how the finished project will look and function. Consider durability, maintenance, and other factors that will affect long-term results. Consider short-term and long-term trends and how they might affect the resale value of your home.

Estimate the amount of money you can afford for the project. You need to be ready in case extra charges become necessary. Some people figure that you should have at least 10 percent more money available than what you think you need.

Usually: "My budget doesn't allow for..." or "We are over budget..." or other similar statements indicate poor planning by the customer.

Use the D.U.E system and be a trustworthy customer. Don't mess up a trustworthy team. Remember that when customers use less than trustworthy tactics, they end up with a less than trustworthy finished project.

It is easy to say that "the general contractor should have made sure every thing was in order," but often the customer is to blame. The customer is the only part of the team that he has no control over.

Trustworthy people will focus fairly. When they hear negative comments about a general contractor or other professional, they will hold judgment until all the facts are in. General contractors and other professionals with established good reputations should always be considered innocent until proven guilty.

Do it right or don't do it.

CLOSING THOUGHTS

As I WROTE this book, editors kept recommending that I shorten it. I did. Then it was requested that I shorten it further. I did. Eventually, it got to a point that I didn't feel comfortable cutting out more. To keep it honest, I focused more on what I think most people need to read and less on what they are use to reading.

As I talk to customers, I notice that it isn't enough to provide advice. Most customers need to be convinced. Repeating my advice and explaining details seems to work. Often I have to disprove bad advice customers got from unreliable sources. Sometimes I have to explain details to illustrate that others oversimplified and misled.

Focus on details concerning the plumber you trust to do work in your home. Focus on details concerning the plumbing products you allow in your home. Focus on details concerning the trustworthiness of the plumbing expert that you trust for advice.

Plumbing products can protect you and your family from very unhealthy living conditions. Proper selection, installation, and maintenance require more than just research-they require proper research. Proper research should save you money and help you avoid overwhelming confusion. Proper research should provide the best chance of achieving the best long-term results.

I hope the advice in this book will help you and your local trustworthy, properly licensed plumber make the best decisions.

Thank you for taking the time to read this, the first of my books. Now, you will find it much easier to gather trustworthy plumbing advice.

Free advice and updates can be found at:

WWW.OnlinePlumbingAdvice.COM

WWW.MikeQuick.COM

www.ingramcontent.com/pod-product-compliance
Lightning Source LLC
Chambersburg PA
CBHW072031080426
42733CB00010B/1855